Questions That Matter

Roger Breisch

Copyright ©2017 Roger Breisch
All rights reserved.

No part of this book may be reproduced, scanned, or distributed in any printed or electronic form without written permission of the publisher.

ISBN: 978-0692920190 (Paperback)

Published by Dancing With Chaos

Dedication

To Judi

M.R.F.L.

Acknowledgements

This work offers ideas, questions and wisdom that have been gifted to me through thousands of teachers. I am thankful to each and every one.

I am grateful to those who have helped me learn through formal instruction—those with whom I agreed, as well as many who gifted me with wisdom that erupted from vehement disagreement. I recall teachers who helped me understand the worth of, and risk involved in, perspectives that question and challenge convention. I cherish their observations and courage. Finally, I am forever indebted to those who recognized my capacities more clearly than I, and challenged me to live into my full potential.

As a teacher, both formally and informally, I am beholden to those who refused to allow me to be satisfied with existing perceptions, opinions and visions. In this book, I suggest that our current thinking is always limited in its ability to help us understand the depth of the human journey. Thank you to those who continually remind me the same limitations are true of my own.

For 15 years I have had the privilege of hosting a Socrates Café. For two hours, twice a month, we invite anyone who is interested to join us as we probe questions that animate our lives. While together, we try to remain "in the question," rather than settling for an easy, convenient answer. Over the years, hundreds have stopped by to test these unusual waters. I am thankful to each of them, but I am most grateful for the group of inquirers who have remained throughout the years. They have not only helped me see deeply, they have become true and trusted friends.

There is a totem I carry: a keychain engraved with the number of hours I have spent answering calls on a depression and suicide hotline. Its most recent entry reads 3000. In those hours, I have been touched by the insights that flow from the hearts of people at the darkest, most frightening moments of  their lives. Each of them has a unique, profound understanding of the human journey—and I have been the recipient of their wisdom.

In 2006, my daughter invited me to join her for a weekend retreat with teens who were part of Operation Snowball, an organization that helps high school students live healthy lives. I have attended two weekend retreats every year since, and hundreds of evening meetings with thousands of astonishing young people. I have no way of knowing if any of these envoys will carry messages from me into the future. However, of this I am certain: hundreds of teens and adults have held up a mirror and asked me to be witness to my own potential and capacity. I am more because of each one of you.

There is only one person I acknowledge by name. This work is dedicated to Judi, the woman I married on June 19, 1982. I have often said that, since I chose her and she chose me, it's clear I have much better taste than she does. The dedication reads "To Judi, M.R.F.L.". Years ago, in a cartoon strip in which two characters were living together, the young man is confused as to how to refer to his partner.

After a moment of confusion compounded by several possibilities, his partner glares in frustration and says, "How about *'your reason for living!'*" In all my years of searching for meaning and wisdom, I know Judi has too often felt she was not the most important thing in my life. But there is nothing I have done, nothing I have learned, no single moment of impact I might have had, that would have happened without her. The journey has not always been easy, but it has been astonishing because of her love, wisdom, insight, belief in me, and support for the countless paths I have traversed. She is, and will always be, my reason for living.

Contents

Introduction 1
   The Subterranean Jungle 10
First Inquiry: The Nature of Knowledge & Wisdom 13
   Confusion on the Journey...19
   Your Brain is Lying to You 23
   Beyond the Finite to the Infinite 27
   Has Knowledge Blinded Us to Wisdom?...............................29
   Learning to Love the Not Knowing..33
   Never Far from Tears 35
Second Inquiry: Questions About Self 39
   Patiently Waiting For Me..43
   Something In Me Will Die...47
   If It Were That Easy… 51
   Allowing You to be You 55
   A Time I Will Not See..57
   On the Eve of an Inventure 61
Third Inquiry: Questions Of & About Others 65
   Nothing Stunning…Really?...73
   Listen and Believe..77
   Sex in a Fishbowl...81
   The Layers of Who We Are Not...85
   Majesty and Radiance..87
   Acknowledging with Grace, Gratitude and Humility 91
   How Are You Doing? 95

Fourth Inquiry: How Might We Live 99
    Godspeed on My Journey 107
    Feather on the Breeze 111
    Surrender...It's Not for the Faint of Heart 115
    Eroding the Riverbanks of Life 117
    The River of Life 121
    On Being Fully Human 123
    A Message 500 Years in the Making 125
    Kicking and Screaming 129
    Regret at the End of Life 131
Fifth Inquiry: Our Individual & Collective Journeys 135
    Orchids and Roses 141
    The Miracle of Life 143
    A Single Day of Eternity 147
    Being Exhausted Before Life Ends 151
    Humanity on the Cusp 155
    Moving to a Different Rock 159
The Continuing Inquiry: Could We See It Another Way? 163
About the Author 169

Introduction

"Would you be willing to share with me, why you want to live?"

This question, asked of those whose lives are so bereft of joy and connection they have considered ending them, has taught me much about life and the human journey.

A young father, through rivers of tears, will tell me he has the most beautiful daughters and cannot imagine inflicting them with the life-long ache that would come from losing the father they love. A woman, bone weary from a life of giving to others, wondering in agony why no one seems willing to give in return, will pause, look deeply inside and declare, "I still have so much left to give." A teen, feeling worthless because of the searing pain that emanates from natural insecurities and false accusations of peers, will admit that perhaps their life is a gift as yet unopened. In those moments, I am moved by the authenticity, vulnerability and wisdom that emerge from human pain and heartache. They also emerge from a sincere and authentic question.

I have come to know the vital role of questions, and grieve the dearth of them in our everyday discourse.

We all have questions about our life, our work, our gifts, our relationships and what, if anything, they mean. We struggle to know how to live in a complex and confusing world. We desperately want to know what the future might bring for us and for humanity. But in this world of to-do lists, action items and requisite answers, we seldom take time to quietly reflect on the deep questions that underlie our existence. Even nature, during the fall and winter, allows times of quiet and rest so new life can germinate and grow. Without time to slow down and reflect, what is new within us, that which yearns to germinate and grow, will, instead, wither and die.

Putting aside deceitful questions—whose cadence and tone imply an answer—all questions matter. Sentences that end with the ubiquitous squiggle atop a period open the future to new possibilities. Sentences ending with just a period condemn the future to limitation and constraint. Answers have a way of ending discovery and learning; captivating questions open us to unimagined possibilities.

The questions that animate our life and language change as age and circumstance evolve. Questions that matter to a child who is just becoming aware of self are different from those of an elder contemplating the end of self. Questions of a young couple newly in love are different from those of a couple whose love may about to be torn asunder by separation, divorce or death. The questions that inform the human species are certainly different today than those we considered 50 years ago, during the Middle Ages, or as we first began to paint symbols on the walls of ancient caves. Regardless of the time of our life, or the eon of the human journey, questions light the way.

Humanity in Transition

Humanity is in the midst of a profound transition, a point of criticality. We are experiencing change more reorienting than the Industrial Revolution, more culture-shattering than the Renaissance and perhaps even more basic and essential than the emergence of human consciousness.

I find myself alive during a time of great discovery—a time when I am being forced to admit that many long-held explanations for reality leave me feeling empty. The logical and scientific solutions to life's mysteries turn out to be something of a shell game. I keep looking under the shells I am certain have the answers, only to be left disappointed when the really deep, difficult questions remain unresolved. The models I have always used to explain the inner workings of the Universe help me negotiate my day-to-day life, but fall short as I ponder questions about who I am and why I am here—questions that have been part of the human experience since time began.

We know that evolution—and most creativity—takes place on the edge between order and chaos. In such a world, life's moments of chaos are just as natural—and necessary—as times of stability and order, yet, we spend much of our time as a species building levees to protect ourselves lest the river of chaos overflow its banks and disrupt our stability. One has only to look at the real levees we've built to stem the natural course of rivers to understand that nature, not humanity, will have its freedom in the end.

I must live in the midst of all this confusion. I wake every morning and move through my days. The way in which I move, the thousands of decisions I make, are all informed by my understanding of self, others and the world around me. The more deeply I am able to peer into the world, the more profound is my experience of it. The depth of my vision is directly related to the number and quality of the questions I ask.

From Whence Do These Questions Come?

I am a learner, and my learning has come from widely diverse life experiences. I am an avid reader. My interests span most aspects of human knowledge. I study mathematics, psychology, physics, spirituality of all varieties, biology, ecology, nature, evolution, the cognitive sciences, leadership, business, indigenous cultures, chaos, complexity and so much more. Many of the questions in this book arise from my interaction with human wisdom as I have encountered it.

I have led an episodic life. The greatest episodes of which, have been as husband, father, son, brother and uncle. I have journeyed professionally through higher education, teaching, business, entrepreneurship and community affairs. As a member of my community, I have had the pleasure of volunteering extensively in the dialogues, debates, hopes and dreams of those with whom I live.

The most profound lessons, those most deeply explored in the pages that follow, are from a study of humanity…at least the humanity close enough to touch my life, my heart and my soul.

For more than 14 years—3000 hours—I have had the privilege of answering calls on a depression and suicide hotline. I have been able to spend many of those hours with humans so confused and distraught by life, they have considered ending theirs. In those difficult moments, they come to understand something precious about the nature of life, and I become the beneficiary of their wisdom. Many of the questions that follow come from that learning.

In addition, more than 11 years ago, when my daughter was in high school, she invited me to accompany her on a weekend teen leadership retreat sponsored by Operation

Snowball. At its heart, Snowball is an anti-drug, anti-alcohol program, but it is designed for any teen who wishes to find a community of peers who want to live healthy lives. When you gather teens, and give them a safe place to speak their truth, it's not long before you deal with sadness, depression, confusion—and, yes, sometimes suicidal thoughts. You will hear their voices, too, in the pages that follow.

More than fourteen years ago, I organized a local Socrates Café as suggested in the book by that name, authored by Christopher Phillips. Since then, twice a month, for two hours, I have had the great joy of pondering with a small group, all of whom have become dear, trusted friends. At the Café, we don't gather to conclude, but rather to include. We take almost any topic—values, the meaning of life, love, the nature of human nature, etc.—and delve deeply into the nuances of these issues to understand them in new and deeper ways. Some of those inquiries show up in these essays.

Finally, through an unlikely turn of events, I led the local Chamber of Commerce for ten years. Chambers of Commerce are a conundrum to most people. Whenever I tried to explain the many roles of such an organization, eyes would glaze over. But in the end, Chambers are associations of humans who are, in an often confusing and difficult world, trying to turn their efforts into a reasonable living for the people they care about. As Executive Director, I fashioned a phrase that captures my view of Chambers of Commerce: "For the life of your business…and the business of your life." The times I felt most passionate and useful in my role were the moments in which a member would generously allow me to help them explore the business of their life…and trust that the life of their business would follow.

All of these places have been pregnant with life itself. And as life has shown up through these many experiences, questions have arisen…and many of them will challenge you in the coming pages.

The Nature of Inquiry

The questions I most love to inhabit are those that, if true, hold the possibility of changing everything I know of the world. I am in love with questions that disrupt; those that perch on the edge of what I currently believe and threaten to nudge me into the great unknown.

These are questions that matter. They rise to the surface in my life because so many of the answers with which I grew up no longer describe the world I have come to know. They are questions of our age; questions we must face as our perceptions of the world and our role in it, are challenged in dramatic ways. How can we discover who we are and what we have to give to the world? Have we given up wisdom by our avoidance of pain, suffering and death? How might we honor our youth and our elders? Has science hidden a deeper order, and deeper wisdom, from us? Will humanity survive and if so, what might be our journey?

It seems many people have such confidence in the answers provided by our current path and myths, they have stopped questioning the most fundamental assumptions underlying them. We seem to have forgotten that one of our unique gifts as conscious beings is our ability and desire to ponder the imponderable, challenge the status quo and alter the paradigms through which we interpret the world.

A Book of Questions...Not Answers

Some time ago, based on a book proposal, I had an opportunity to meet with an experienced publisher. It was a short and difficult summit. "Roger," he told me kindly, "you're a good writer, but I can't publish the book you have proposed. Few people read entire books anymore and too many of your ideas come far too late in the volume. Your readers want to know what you have to say in the first few pages. The rest of the book is for examples and clarification, but don't expect anyone to read it." He pointed me to one very successful book he had recently published that revealed its message in the title. You needn't even open to page one.

I was crestfallen. Perhaps I'm arrogant, but I believed my thoughts and ideas too numerous, too deeply philosophical, too personal, and too diverse to be wrapped neatly into the few hundred words that might begin a work. I've contemplated many book ideas, but always came up short when I believed I had to force my ideas into some simple, overarching theme.

What I have done for many years is to craft short essays, each of which explores a topic that animates me, and raises questions in that moment. What drives me is not a single topic or well-defined set of ideas, but numerous diverse ideas and questions with the potential to drive a wedge into everything I thought I understood.

So rather than try to force my thinking and essays into a well-structured, singular flow of thought, I chose to focus on the only thread they all share: the power and authority of the questions they raise. I chose to share them as they exploded from me, allowing them to remain as they were birthed. They had power and energy for me as they arrived, and they lost that power when I tried to fit them into some thematic mold. Our two children are unique and beautiful exactly as they are. It would seem violent to make them fit a mold in which they did not belong. (See "Orchids and Roses" in the Fifth Inquiry.) These essays too, were birthed as individuals and it would seem violent to rip their individuality from them by aligning them just to fit a theme.

I have instead, organized them into five inquiries. But make no mistake, they are inquiries…not answers. Each of the five topics have been explored through the ages. Millions of words, thousands of books, have been written about each. I hold no pretense that I have explored any of them in a complete way. My hope is that they raise even more questions, not provide answers. Questions open us to new futures, answers bound and limit the future. My deepest hope is that this entire volume enters your life as a question. If the questions herein have any veracity, many will leave you confused and even disturbed. Confusion, being lost, it is said, is an integral part of the human journey.

The First Inquiry is an exploration of the nature of knowledge and wisdom. It would seem arrogant to comment on epistemology, one of the most examined issues of all time. My essays are not meant to add, critique or alter the insights of those who come before. They are simply intended to share the questions that arise in my life about the nature of knowledge and wisdom. What is knowledge? Are there limits to what we could know? Is it possible knowledge can prevent us from finding wisdom? In this culture, I fear, knowledge in the moment is power, and the wisdom that emerges across time and that which is available only through profound, unanswerable questions, plays a secondary role.

The Second Inquiry is a compilation of essays in which I explore the questions that bound my own existence, or at least what I think I know of my existence. How do I know who I am? How do I discern others' visions of me, and in what ways do I reconcile that difference between the self I see...and the person you perceive? Confusion reigns as my sense of self morphs throughout my life.

In the Third Inquiry, I reveal questions I have asked of and about others, and what those questions have taught me about what it means to be human. How do we see others, and how do those views impact our view of self? It can be difficult to reconcile the stories that leave us feeling inadequate with the views of others who experience our majesty and radiance.

The Fourth Inquiry explores what it means to live a life of value. How do we spend the moments we have been given on this planet? Do we create beauty and leave value in our wake? A question I have always loved is, how do I know if the life I am living is my life? How do I know if I am living in the best way possible in the years I have been given?

The Fifth Inquiry contains essays about our individual and collective journeys. What, in the end, might they mean? Now that modern medicine has enabled us to push death to the further reaches of life, do we value life less? Do we expect far too much from our time on this planet regardless of our life expectancy? What of the human species in its journey on the planet? Do we act as though we truly belong? I have written in this section about many questions I find deeply troubling.

I conclude the introduction with a favorite piece, based on a question from many years ago, that pointed me in the direction of all that follows.

The Subterranean Jungle

Many years ago, I taught in a private high school on the outskirts of Princeton, New Jersey. As faculty advisor in the dorm, I began each day at breakfast with the students. One freshman would frequently catch me in the dining room. "Mr. Breisch, may I ask you a question?" I'd reply, "You just did! Would you like to ask another?" At the time, I felt our early morning repartee was nothing more than a way to point out a bit of irony he seemed unable to grasp. I now believe he was pointing me towards my future ... a future in which life's questions have become infinitely important, and answers are often more destructive than constructive.

So, even though we are not in line awaiting breakfast, may I ask a question? Or two? Have we lost the art of assembling provocative words into questions that inquire into the great mysteries of the Universe? To what extent do the answers we summon imprison our thinking and hold it hostage? When was the last time you heard a question so profound it left you in wonderment and awe? How often, in the face of questions, do we find ourselves in search of the nearest convenient answer, regardless of its ability to add a bit of wisdom to the human narrative? How often do we formulate questions for which we truly have no answer, as opposed to those whose sole purpose is to allow us to loose a carefully crafted declarative response?

Questions open us to possibilities; answers limit the future. Nowhere is this more clear than when facing a caller on the suicide hotline. In the presence of extreme desperation, would you more likely be called into a deeper conversation by a declaration such as "Suicide is not the answer." or by an inquiry like "Would you be willing to share with me why you want to live?"

Lest you think my wandering through the subterranean jungle of human conversation relates only to deeply philosophical questions, or those regarding the end of life, allow me to stroll through a few of the forests that more often characterize day-to-day life.

In conversations with my wife and children I find myself too willing to jump in with a statement ending in a period, often a very large period at that. I wonder how our lives might have evolved differently if, when faced with a thought I found difficult to accept, I might respond with "That's *very* interesting. Would you tell me more?"

Over the years, I have listened as many community issues have traveled the highways and byways of our public discourse. After acrimonious debate, we decided we did not want a hotel on a thoroughfare near a neighborhood, but we would permit a shopping center on a portion of a marsh that many felt should remain open space. We elected not to decide the fate of a dam on a local river. Even now we find ourselves in the midst of difficult deliberations regarding the master plan for our downtown and have begun to take sides on the future of a forest preserve just north of the city.

Because of my unique position near the center of many debates, I am often privy to the edges that bound the questions. As I have listened over the years, I have been struck by the dearth of sentences that end with a question mark. Our "public hearings" are too often attended by people who have stopped listening.

The word "discussion" itself calls into question our intentions. Its evolution from Latin meant to "smash apart" or to "scatter and disperse." Shouldn't our community conversations begin with an intention to gather our ideas in a generative fashion rather than scatter and disperse them?

In the coming years, humanity will face moral and ethical issues more profound than any we have ever faced. Brain scans will allow us to know what others are thinking, thus obliterating even the most intimate forms of human privacy. Genetics will allow us to custom design our children. The harvesting of human organs will blur the line between life and death. These deeply challenging issues will require intricate, new answers. Unless these answers are preceded by the most profound questions we can conjure, I fear we will be forever lost in the subterranean jungle.

First Inquiry:
The Nature of Knowledge & Wisdom

"The modern mind has lost all capacity to wonder. It has lost all capacity to look into the mysterious, into the miraculous—because of knowledge, because it thinks it knows. The moment you think you know, wonder stops arising. The moment you start becoming less knowledgeable, wonder comes back, starts penetrating you."[1]

    Osho

My first encounter with the idea that knowledge interrupts wonder was many years ago when given the book *Think on these Things,* authored by Jiddu Krishnamurti. I recall being stunned by the idea that every thought imprisons us. Any bit of knowledge, especially that of which we are certain, makes us blind or oblivious to other ways of seeing. Mark Twain once wrote, "It ain't what you don't know that gets you into trouble. It's what you know for sure that just ain't so!"

The gray matter that makes up the control center of my existence is composed of perhaps 100 billion cells and trillions of synapses. The pathways determined by those synapses determine who I am, what I think, what I know, and control how I turn all of that into a meaningful life. Those synapses and neuronal pathways are formed by the very experience of life. From the moment of conception, the experiences of life formed my way of thinking, and that way of thinking has then had a dramatic impact on how I experience life. When considered in those terms, it's a bit of a closed loop. It is difficult, perhaps impossible, to form

---

[1] Zen: The Path of Paradox, Osho. ©2001, Osho International Foundation, St Martin's Press

thought patterns based on experiences that are simply unavailable to us.

So a simple question emerges: how can we be sure the thoughts in our brains are correct? If, by dint of some bit of science fiction, we could have grown up in a truly alien world, is it possible we might see the Universe in a wholly different way? Might we have different explanations for how and why things are the way they are? Might we have a very different understanding of how we came to be and why we might be here? Might our relationships with one another be of a completely different texture?

I needn't be born into an alien world to understand the limits of the things I call knowledge. As I ponder, I realize knowledge is fragile. Over my lifetime, I have been forced to rewire my brain multiple times as my understanding of the Universe, and my role in it, morphs. And, if I am honest, the wiring I now rely on to help me navigate life—knowledge that today seems solid and immutable—will undoubtedly morph even further should I be gifted with a few more years on this human journey.

I often wonder how limited my thinking truly is—despite the feeling that my thoughts are becoming better and more refined. What if they are not? What if the way I think is destined to be always limited in scope, off-kilter in orientation and misguided in direction?

Je pense, donc je suis

The mathematician and philosopher René Descartes first wrote this French phrase in his 1637 "Discourse on the Method". It was translated in Latin as *cogito ergo sum*, and into English as "I think, therefore I am". From that moment forward, perhaps more than any other, emerged a deeply held belief that who I am is synonymous with what emerges from the neurons, axons and synapses of my brain. Perhaps our current interpretation of Descartes' maxim is better stated as "I think, therefore that is who I am." Through all the years of school, I was evaluated on the quality and depth of my logic, rationalizations and declarations. I don't recall getting a single grade for the depth of my feelings, or the quality and profundity of my questions.

Author and social scientist, Brené Brown, says we believe we are intellectual beings who occasionally have an emotional experience. In reality, she says, the reverse is true—we are emotional beings who occasionally have an intellectual experience.

What if our deepest, most profound wisdom is hidden in our hearts, not in the nooks and crannies of our grey matter? Could it be that what is most true about our lives, the world, the biosphere, and the entire Universe emerges in such ubiquitous, subtle, silent ways that we have ceased to hear them? Could it be these truths are beyond the limited facility of words, and the moment we try to capture them in that way, we lose their infinite, deeply profound nature?

The essays in this First Inquiry touch on the many questions that swirl around the theme of human knowledge and wisdom.

"Confusion on the Journey" questions the very basic foundations of my beliefs. Human understanding of the world has changed dramatically in the brief span of my life. I understood atoms and molecules as solid and discrete until quantum particles questioned that very nature. I came to question the role of dreams, the nature of reality, the superiority of the human species, and so much more. All this causes me to wonder about the answers I thought I had for life's most compelling questions, and about the answers I am now living into.

"Your Brain is Lying to You," recalls that much of what we know today is different from what we, as individuals, knew a few years ago, and from what we, as a species, knew a half century or more ago. If you woke every morning with the clear understanding that an enormous slice of the ideas, thoughts and beliefs you held were wrong, how might you be different in the world? To some that thought is terrifying…to others intriguing. To you?

In "Beyond the Finite to the Infinite" I wonder if there is an infinite "out there" to which I am blind because of paradigms that keep me trapped in the finite. And yet, it is precisely those paradigms that challenge me to see beyond them. It leaves me with a deeply confusing paradox: even the idea that my current thinking is limited is itself a limiting paradigm.

Related to that, in "Has Knowledge Blinded Us to Wisdom," I refer to books I have read that ask me to unbelieve so much of what I have been taught to believe. Having married into a family several generations in Hawai'i, and having studied some ancient Hawai'ian wisdom, many of my basic understandings of the world have been called into question. Could spontaneous healing be a reality? Can humans project themselves to different places or levitate their bodies? Can humans survive long periods without food or water? Do I believe these truths? Sometimes I simply choose not to disbelieve.

In 2015, I was invited to speak at TEDxIIT. The event, and the people who surrounded me with love and support changed my life. However, my thinking about the nature of knowledge and wisdom was altered even more. "Never Far from Tears" documents the journey I traveled that keeps me torn between the knowledge of my brain and that of my heart. I wonder if it's true that the heart is the only organ strong enough to educate the mind.

Finally, in the essay "Learning to Love the Not Knowing" I wonder if it's possible that all human knowledge is infinitesimally small in comparison to what might yet be known. I ask perhaps the most ambitious question of all: Is it possible we will someday discover that reality is so far beyond any potential human capability we will find our most enduring satisfaction and happiness in the *not* knowing?

Confusion on the Journey

The more I learn, the more the explanations I grew up with are being called into question—like mental and emotional rugs being yanked out from under me. For every book or article that proposes one worldview, there is another equally well-documented volume to propose another, often contradictory, view. I wonder if reality exists, or which author's reality makes the most sense. Then I wonder if sense-making is even what I should be seeking. I wonder if I know anything at all. Are there really any pillars of truth on which I can build my belief systems?

I grew up in a world composed of atoms and molecules that were substantial, measurable particles. I grew into a Universe of quantum entities that zip in and out of existence at a whim, and show up as particles or waves depending on how we observe them.

I grew up in a world of answers and certainty—a world frightened by questions and confusion. I grew into a Universe in which things like Heisenberg's Uncertainty Principle guarantee I can never have all the answers. Knowledge of one aspect of the Universe makes another unknowable. I have come to learn that answers have a way of ending discovery and learning—while captivating questions open us to possibilities.

I grew up in a world in which my existence was primarily biological. My soul had a clean slate and one shot, using this body only, to make or break its infinite future in either heaven or hell. I grew into a Universe with legitimate discussion of my soul's journey through many lifetimes to continue its growth in wisdom and enlightenment.

I grew up in a world where nature versus nurture was the only disagreement about how I came to be the person I am. I grew into a Universe in which some, like psychologist James Hillman and author Gary Zukav, suggest that my soul chose this life, with its possibilities for both joy and pain, because of the work it had to do in order to continue its journey.

I grew up in a world in which dreams were the random firings of 100 billion neurons that yielded meaningless images to be ignored, laughed at or forgotten. I grew into a Universe in which dreams might contain information about what I am called to do, or messages with deep meaning for my life's journey. My children used Native American dream catchers to keep bad dreams out of their lives, rather than for their original purpose—to capture the meaning of dreams for insight about one's life and calling.

I grew up on a planet large enough to have an "other side." I grew into a Universe where communication technology, especially the Internet, invites the entire world into my living room. The "other side" is now on this side.

I grew up in a world where the American way of life was the envy of all. Consumerism and our market economy were great gifts that had the potential to make every human wealthy. I grew into a Universe in which it is increasingly clear there aren't nearly enough resources to raise the world's living standards to those of the United States. Our wasteful ways are raising the global temperature and destroying large portions of the biosphere and may eventually even extinguish the human species.

I grew up in a world in which every theory, supposition, and belief had, at its heart, the fundamental importance, intelligence and superiority of humanity. Our extraordinary talents and abilities would eventually, I was led to believe, enable us to remake this place into a safe, risk-free and stable home for humans. We either were, or soon would be, the masters of all we surveyed. I grew into a Universe in which order is inherent—order that contains chaos as an integral component—and this orderliness does not require humanity to hold it together or build on it. Not only are we not required, we may be superfluous!

I grew up in a world where lives could be planned and made predictable. It was my job as a youth to find the right career so I could support a certain and stable family. Middle age was for amassing wealth because money was the only route to a bright and happy retirement. I grew into a Universe where the wisest, most deeply spiritual people I know live lives that show up in unexpected ways because they listen carefully to what they are called to do. Their lives are unpredictable and unplanned—filled with terrifying uncertainty, profound confusion...and deep satisfaction. They live lives with unimaginable wealth—sometimes they even have money.

I am slipping from youth to old age with the fear that somewhere along the way, I was supposed to have found wisdom—answers to life's deep and imponderable questions. What I have learned is that the answers become more elusive with age and the questions grow in number and complexity.

I am a man with significant formal education who knows that his most precious and profound learning was uncovered outside the classroom.

I am a former teacher who discovered that it was not the content, but the context of my relationships with young people that had the greatest impact. And it was they who were the teachers and I the reluctant student.

I am a former manager from a Fortune 500 company who left because there seemed little room for humanity...little time in between sales calls, business meetings and strategy sessions for us to discover who we are as human beings or what we long for. Too much of the conversation was about a bigger bottom line and higher ROI, and not enough about building a spiritual legacy for future generations. There was too much of the masculine voice of decision-making and action planning and not enough of the feminine voice calling us to meaning through relationship.

It is a deeply confusing time. I have many "answers" for the challenges I face. The irony is that most of those answers only work in the world in which I grew up. They are often useless in the Universe into which I grew. The confusion is often so intense I find myself on early-morning walks moving moment-to-moment from despair to joy, terror to ecstasy, sadness to deep gratitude, with tears running down my face to signify any and all of these emotions. I wonder what I am called to think...to believe...to do. While the world offers many "answers" to each of my myriad questions, I know that few will work. I must find my own. I know where I have been—or at least I think I do—but I am profoundly confused about where I am headed.

Your Brain is Lying to You

You don't have to agree with my premise, however, if I propose a thought experiment, would you play along for just a moment?

Starting right now, suppose you knew for a fact that a significant portion—perhaps 30, 40 or 50 percent—of everything you thought, felt and believed was wrong, or at least considerably askew. Further, what if everyone else had the same awareness of their own thoughts and feelings? How might you, each day, enter the world differently? I have been asking this question in recent presentations, and the conclusions vary wildly.

Some find the idea horrifying: "I'd never be able to make a decision." "I would be frightened to say anything." "I think I would be paralyzed." "We'd never get anything done!"

Many find it reassuring: "I'd be more curious, less dogmatic." "I would ask more questions." "I would enter the world more gently." "I'd be more open to learning."

Admittedly, I fall into this latter category.

Too often, in today's public discourse, the retort to an opposing view often sounds like "You're an idiot, and let me tell you why." We have public hearings in which, I fear, no one is listening. Attend one sometime and see if you can discern any question marks hiding out amongst the very large and forceful periods that end most sentences. Of course you'll have to discount "questions" the likes of *"Are you nuts?"*

The world would be a better place if each of us opened ourselves first to the possibility of our own rational shortcomings, rather than clawing desperately for the flaw in the logic of others. If I was truly interested in listening for my shortcomings, rather than yours, might it become a more thoughtful, sympathetic world imbued with greater understanding? But then, attention to my own failings would require courage...and a less tenacious ego.

Having read a great deal about our current understanding of the human brain, there are overwhelming reasons to accept the premise that a significant percent of a human's thoughts is misguided.

Human memory is imprecise and capricious. Your brain dissects experiences and stores them in disparate parts of your cortex. When memories are recalled, these pieces are reassembled, not accurately, but in a "good-enough" fashion that is easily distorted. Eyewitness accounts in a court of law, we now know, are among the least reliable pieces of evidence. Once a supposed culprit is identified in a sketchbook or lineup, that image replaces the one real one formed in the cortex at the moment of the offense.

Have you ever jumped to conclusions about another human being based on how they dress, a bumper sticker on their car, a sound bite or rumor...only to discover you pre-judged them erroneously?

How much of what you believe today is identical with what you believed 10 or 20 years ago? While some new thinking is based on adding to your store of knowledge, haven't you discovered many ways in which your thinking in years past was inaccurate?

How much of what humankind believes today is the same as we believed, say, 500 years ago? I dare say very little. Is it possible what we believe 500 years from now will be equally distant from what we "know" is true today? I think it is.

So, is it conceivable that 10 or 20 years from now, each of us will, in fact, discover that some large portion of our beliefs today are limited, misguided or flat out wrong? I hope so! Put another way: in 10 years, if I am destined to think *exactly* as I do today…just shoot me now!

But, then again, I'm probably wrong about this whole idea.

Beyond the Finite to the Infinite

As I reflect on the human journey, today is the eve of Easter, the most holy of holy days on the Christian calendar. I am informed, and confused, by words attributed to Jesus as he neared death: *"Eli, Eli, lama sabachthani?"* that is, "My God, My God, why hast Thou forsaken Me?" In this moment, I wonder if even Jesus, who tradition tells us could see beyond the reality of this world—what I call the finite—into the Infinite, had moments of doubt about the Infinite? In his excruciating moment of pain it would not be surprising if even Jesus' understanding of the Infinite was obfuscated by his experience of the finite?

Even though I hope never to experience the finite in that same horrific way, I wonder if the Infinite is hidden from me also by my experience of the finite. For more than 60 years I have read hundreds of books that attempt to describe this world—from Quantum Physics, Evolutionary Biology and Moral Psychology to Buddhism, Confucianism and New Age Spirituality. Each contains an explanation of what this world really is, and why we are here. What if every explanation we attempt actually prevents us from seeing what is beyond them?

I have come to believe the Universe is ineffable—beyond words. It is beyond anything we can understand from the perspective of the finite. And yet, we continue to manufacture concepts, images and paradigms to help us understand that which is ineffable. What if, instead of helping us understand, the paradigms obfuscate, distort and confuse?

What if we are actually in the Infinite—what many refer to as Heaven—right now, but are unable to see it, or experience it, because we remain so confused by what our minds think we are supposed to see? What if nothing I see is what I think it is? What if life has been gifted to me, not to comprehend the finite, but as a brief opportunity for me to see that what lies beyond is not beyond at all, but right in front of me, concealed by my thinking? But then, that too would be a paradigm, perhaps also keeping me from witnessing what is beyond. It is as if the paradigms that make up my world keep me locked in this place…keep me from the Infinite. It is as if, every time I try to see beyond, another view from the finite reflects me back to this world and this place.

Hundreds of teachers ask me to see that life is in being, not doing. They encourage me to see this moment—as I allow life to be lived through me and, to the extent I can, give up my ego—as filled with grace. It is in not knowing that I even glimpse what might be beyond the finite. The Buddha would have called this Beginner's Mind. True knowledge is not found by thinking, I am instructed. But how do I approach their thinking, if it is about the non-belief in thoughts? Is it permissible to use thoughts to get beyond thought? All truly is paradox. Yet somehow I feel that beyond the paradox…beyond the thinking…beyond the paradigms is the Infinite.

If the wisdom of the ages is to let go of all, to stop trying and simply be, then the ultimate paradox, the meta-paradigm if you will, is that it has taken so many words, concepts and paradigms for me to see that the Infinite is only available when I let go of all that led me to this moment.

Has Knowledge Blinded Us to Wisdom?

If I am open to the road less traveled, life lies in wait to take me on extraordinary journeys. A recent such escapade began in the most unlikely of places—with an obscure comment in Walter Isaacson's biography of Steve Jobs. Isaacson mentions, in passing, a book Jobs reportedly reread every year. It wasn't a book on technology, or one that explored business, economics, product design, politics, movies or music. It was an autobiography written by a Hindu spiritual figure first published in 1946. Just before departing for our recent vacation to Hawai'i, I purchased *Autobiography of a Yogi* by Paramahansa Yogananda. I turned the final page as the plane hit the tarmac in Honolulu. It was clear the road forward was about to take a radical turn—as I caught sight of the ancient volcanoes that formed the beautiful island of O'ahu, Yogananda's work pointed me to three ancient texts: *The Bhagavad Gita, The Upanishads* and *The Way of the Bodhisattva.*

These volumes are wonderfully disturbing. Wonderful, because, if I am open to the messages they offer, the Universe becomes a larger and more interesting place. Yogananda recounts times in which spiritual teachers would accurately foretell the future, live for months or years without eating or drinking, spontaneously heal those who were ill, levitate their bodies many feet off the ground and simultaneously appear in more than one place. I find these books disturbing because every neuron in my brain fights back, having been wired and rewired by western science. They collectively scream, *"You cannot believe any of this…and even if you do, you better not admit it to anyone!"* The culture in which I was raised would have me pass these texts and ideas off as fantasy, fiction, witchcraft or perhaps even psychoses.

It might be possible to put the books of Indian & Tibetan Hinduism aside as a collection of wayward thought. But then I recall a surprise discovery in my father-in-law's library shortly after he died in 1999. There, amongst his books, lay many that recounted the spiritual traditions of the ancient Hawai'ians. Their spiritual leaders and healers were called *kahuna*. The kahuna, like the swamis and yogis of Hinduism, also performed many clearly impossible acts. There are those in Hawai'i who, to this day, will talk, for example, of witnessing spontaneous healing of human ailments.

Should you choose to set aside both Hawai'ian and Hindu spiritual tradition in order to hold sacred the wisdom of Western science and technology, then be prepared to set aside the ancient traditions of many of the indigenous peoples of the world—Africa, South America, Australia and others. It's safe and easy to set all this "witchcraft" aside, and reflect exclusively upon the enlightenment heralded by the coming of Aristotle and western logic, science and analysis. I, on the other hand, wonder if I should be more open to rewiring my neural connections to allow the possibility of perception in radically new ways.

On a long walk up the ancient, extinct volcanoes of Hawai'i, I recounted some of the stories I was reading to my daughter. "Do you believe them?" she asked. "At this moment," I told her, "I am choosing not to disbelieve…to remain uncertain." Because if the certainty of western knowledge has left me blind to—unable or unwilling to see—the reality of wisdom traditions that are broader, more complex, mysterious and infinitely more interesting, I want the possibility of being a witness to those traditions in the few years I have left in this life.

    I wonder if, that too, was the road Steve Jobs traveled.

Learning to Love the Not Knowing

Neil Armstrong, on his return from the moon said "It suddenly struck me that that tiny pea, pretty and blue, was the Earth. I put up my thumb and shut one eye, and my thumb blotted out the planet Earth. I didn't feel like a giant. I felt very, very small."

What if the same were true of human knowledge? What if all human knowledge could, metaphorically, be hidden behind a carefully placed thumb? What if the entirety of human thought is similarly small in relation to the vast innate wisdom that permeates the Universe? What if, in reality, we actually understand very little? What then? What do we do? How should we act, if we must proceed into the next moment with the understanding that we have little understanding? If true, this might be one of the greatest of human paradoxes.

There are, I believe, reasons to question the scope of human knowledge.

The Universe is 14 billion years in the making—the Earth some 4.5 billion—yet we believe we have come close to understanding its deepest secrets in the four or five hundred years since Galileo, Newton and Descartes. On this trajectory, if we complete our understanding in the next two hundred years, or, being conservative, one thousand, what then for the rest of humanity's future? Will there be nothing for them to ponder about the Universe and how it works?

Even worse, what if our "knowledge" actually drags us further and further from the infinity of the Universe? Is there a possibility our thinking is so mired in orthodoxy we can no longer see beyond the limits of our current beliefs? What if, by insisting we only look through certain lenses, we are becoming more and more blind rather that more and more wise?

Is it possible that 1000 years from now, rather than having used the scientific method to find ultimate answers, we will have set aside that entire belief system as an infinitely constricted lens into the nature of reality? Might we eventually come to understand that any human view of reality will one day be similarly viewed as infinitely constricted? Is it possible we will someday discover that reality is so far beyond any potential human capability we will find our most enduring satisfaction and happiness in the not knowing?

I believe humans will always be in love with the search for the most profound wisdom the Universe is willing to share. So in love, in fact, that if we discover the deepest wisdom comes from not knowing, we will learn to love the not knowing.

Never Far from Tears

I have spoken before larger audiences, but this was to be my first TEDx talk. Giving such a talk is a huge honor, but, at some point you realize your remarks will live forever on the Internet; it matters not whether you deliver them with eloquence...or stumble meaninglessly for 18 minutes. The thought of reliving a poor performance for the rest of one's life can add a certain amount of terror to the moment.

As I drafted, edited and practiced my remarks, my hope was to influence those who might eventually hear them. I had a number of groups willing to hear what was on my mind in the weeks preceding TEDxIIT, so I had abundant opportunities to rehearse. I discovered, as the ideas rewrote themselves, the more I spoke from my heart, the stronger the reaction to my message. When I edged towards a logical, rational narration, the audience responded with polite applause and kind comments. When I spoke from my heart, with words tinted by emotion, those to whom I spoke reacted with rapt attention and walked away with deeper understanding. They found within, and shared with each other, more profound wisdom.

The journey I traversed in the 24 hours before my walk onto that stage is worth a comment so I can honor the person who gave me permission to think from my heart...to navigate the territory between logic and emotion with deep authenticity in that very public, frightening place.

The fourteen presenters rehearsed the day before TEDxIIT. After my rehearsal, Bob, the stage manager and advisor, pulled me aside and admitted my remarks touched him. He is a professional speaker and actor—his command of the stage is inspiring—so his generous comment helped build my confidence and allay the terror. However, as the conference began the following day, my trepidation grew. Since many of the talks preceding mine had a decidedly technical bent, I feared the audience would be uninterested in my message. My remarks were written to educate their mind by touching their hearts.

At the break, I told Bob I was losing my nerve. When I expressed my fear the audience was in a state of mind rather than a state of heart, he told me "What you have to say is more important than any of the technology stuff." It was kind and generous, but not nearly as powerful as the words he imparted the moment before I walked on the stage. He grabbed me by the arm, looked me in the eye and said, "You go out there and make me cry!"

From the first moments on that stage, as I mentioned my work on the suicide hotline, I wrestled with tears. I wondered if I touched on my emotions too early, but as I walked off the stage, Bob reassured me once again. "Did you see the audience's reaction? You grabbed their attention from those early moments and never let go."

Someone once said the heart is the only organ strong enough to educate the mind. A number of years ago, when improvisational pianist Michael Jones (See the essay "Nothing Stunning…Really?" in the Third Inquiry.) reminded me of that wisdom, he added, "When we are thinking from our heart we are never far from tears."

I frequently find myself betwixt and between logical thought and deep emotion; caught somewhere in the fissure between my cerebral cortex and my heart. We live in an era that would have us believe the logical and rational are the singular keys to success. We practically abhor emotions. When they arrive, often unbidden, we are encouraged not to feel. One young man I spoke with last year was suffering from a number of reversals in his life. He was struggling mightily, and told me tearfully how frightened he was. When I asked if he could gain support and comfort from his father and older brother, he said, "You don't understand, in my family, a man who admits to a struggle is simply ridiculed."

The word courage and the word heart both derive from the Latin word *cor*. It takes courage to allow the heart to educate the mind. Perhaps someday we will, collectively, become more comfortable thinking from our hearts...and honor those who are never far from tears.

Second Inquiry: Questions About Self

> *"Your analysis of your life and its failures has the ring of truth since congruent with your self-preoccupation."*

This comment appeared unbidden on my blog. It evoked a great deal of thought and reflection about what occupies my life…and what should. It is critical to listen to those who love us, but we must also heed those who come into our lives unbidden and challenge us to see the world anew. Deep reflection on the unbidden can yield dramatic shifts in our paradigms.

My first reaction was colored by fear and humiliation, with various shades of self-recrimination. I have a deep-seated, private fear that too much of my life has been about, well, my life.

As I continued to reflect, I recalled that preoccupy means to occupy your mind and life with one thing before you live into and contemplate alternatives. If self-preoccupation means to focus on self before others, at first blush, a person who does that would seem to lack humility and regard for others. Certainly that is worthy of self-condemnation!

However, just after I received this missive from cyberspace, I began reading Martin Buber's *I and Thou*. Early in the work Buber says "The basic word I-You can only be spoken with one's whole being."

Perhaps I am a slow learner, but much of what I know of who I am, and who I am capable of being, has come to me in the most recent years of my life. As I have come to discover fragments that lay shy and hidden for nearly half a century, admittedly, I have spent many hours reflecting on, and writing about, the magnitude, boundaries, and meaning of those newly-exposed facets of self.

Is it possible, I began to wonder, that without sufficient occupation with self before others, I am incapable of speaking with my whole being? Is it possible that, without some amount of self-preoccupation I am speaking largely from a false self? Do I need to know self before I can be in relation to others in the sense Buber suggests?

What I have come to believe is that the more I come to know who I am, and of what I am capable, the more easily I can let go of self-preoccupation and relax into being who I was always meant to become.

The essays in the Second Inquiry touch on a few of the many ways I have come to know self, and the ways in which I show up in the lives of others.

"Patiently Waiting for Me" explores my confusion about how I become who I become. If, as I suggest, life is willing to wait for me to become, do I accomplish that by making myself into something, or, instead, by uncovering the deep pieces of who I always was meant to become. Do I write the life of my choosing by etching whatever I wish onto a clean slate, or learn to reveal the person I was sent here to become? How do I find out?

Then, in "Something In Me Will Die," I explore how I might tease out the true me in the face of critiques from others that may pull me away from my essence. How do I know when to honor the critique of a friend or loved one by altering my self-knowledge, and when do I, instead, honor the true self I have come to know?

"If It Were That Easy..." examines the fragility of self-worth. I often talk with people on the suicide hotline who feel they have let themselves down. Some event from their past leaves them horrified by the person they see when they look in the mirror. One young man, only 16, told me, in those moments, he hates everything he sees. And yet, callers disclose, they would easily forgive a friend or loved one who committed the same transgression. How, I wonder, might we give ourselves that same love and generosity we give others?

"Allowing You to be You" recounts a moment many years ago in which I realized I had created a story of someone else's life because it reinforced an inaccurate vision of my own. How often, I wonder, do I limit who I might become by making another human being into a person they are not? By fixing them into some immutable position in the firmament of humanity, do I limit my own possibilities?

In "On the Eve of an Inventure," I reflected on an upcoming retreat with 130 teens. I thought a great deal about what wisdom I might impart on them during the weekend, only to realize that that is precisely the wrong question. Teaching, I came to realize, is far more about who I am than what I say. In the end, I wonder how I might honor the sacredness in them by learning to honor that which is in me.

Finally, "A Time I Will Not See," is an intimate conversation between myself and the young man I was many years ago. A pencil sketch of me as a senior in high school helps me to question who I am becoming, and if I am living into the messages the elders in my life left with me.

Patiently Waiting For Me

"Finally I see...life has been patiently waiting for me"
From the song "I'm Movin' On" by Rascal Flatts

The song "I'm Movin' On" and I had simultaneously visited the same space many times, but being in the same place with an idea, or person, does not mean you are friends...or even acknowledge one another's presence. It certainly does not mean you are in love. But one morning I began a love affair with the words "life has been patiently waiting for me." I have learned to listen carefully when words touch my heart, and those surely did.

The more I reflect on them, the more hopeful, valued and beautifully incomplete I felt. The hope comes from the sense that, even as I bid adieu to middle-age and approach elderhood, life was still willing to wait for me. I am not too late. I feel valued because I am important enough to be waited for, and I am not being waited for by something insignificant—life itself is waiting! Finally, I feel beautifully incomplete! Yes, beautifully incomplete. To be complete would imply there was nothing left to my life. Nothing left to learn. No one left for me to touch, or to be touched by. Incomplete never felt so wonderful.

Or so confusing and frightening.

Questions emerge! Who is the "me" life is waiting patiently for? If I am incomplete, are there parts nearing completion? Are there parts I have yet to even begin to know? If I "know" many things about who I am, can I be certain which are real and which are impostors? How, over the course of my lifetime have I learned to tell the real from the false...the identities that are me, versus those my ego inappropriately apprehended many years ago and is unwilling to release?

There seem endless questions, but one in particular captures me. The "me" life is waiting for...is it someone I have within my power to create, as a sculptor fashioning form out of amorphous clay? Or is life waiting for me to reveal and live into the person I was always meant to be, as a landscape is revealed when curtains are parted? These suddenly seemed two very different views of what it means to grow as a human: to sculpt a person I envision, or to reveal the person envisioned from beyond.

I wonder whether a very common vision of human life—perhaps the pervasive Western view—is wrong, or at least horribly incomplete. I was raised to believe that humans are born *"tabula rasa"*—we arrive as a clean slate on which our story is written and we are the primary authors. Born as nothing more than potential, we are presented with an untold number of years on this Earth during which to create ourselves. "You can be whatever you want to be," I was told in so many ways...and by so many people. The evidence they use to prove that life works this way can be compelling. Look at the legions of role models whose lives seem to verify that worldview—politicians, entrepreneurs, religious leaders and community organizers who made something of themselves. The story line is that through their effort they made themselves into something they would not have been if they had not carefully sculpted it from an amorphous presence.

I am no longer certain that is life's most compelling story.

And what might be a different story of life? A story of emergence more than one of creation. I wonder if life is about growing into who we are meant to be rather than creating who we wish to become. I wonder if life is about allowing the core of who we are to emerge. Taking a metaphor from nature, an oak tree emerges—it does not create itself. A rose blossoms, it doesn't endeavor to be something other than what it is destined to become.

The image I have in mind is that Roger Breisch has, and has had since conception—or earlier—unique strengths, characteristics, personality traits, and gifts, as well as deficits and weaknesses. The perfect descriptors escape me. Regardless, what's important is that the quality of my impact on the world is in direct relation to the extent to which I show up through those gifts and weaknesses—naked and absolutely authentic. To the extent I insist on showing up without them, to the extent I try to co-create the world with those around me as someone I truly am not, I am lost, ineffective and superficial.

There is perhaps a different way of envisioning the metaphor of the sculptor...different from one who creates. I have heard it said that Michelangelo was asked how he could find the magnificent image of David within an amorphous block of stone. As I recall the story, he said the task was easy...he simply chipped away the parts that did not look like David. That is an image of discovery, not one of creation. Perhaps that is a more powerful way of envisioning our lives...as a process of chipping away the parts of the stone that no longer look, or feel, like us.

That is a life-long, difficult task. I trust that life has enough patience.

Something In Me Will Die

Once again, my ego is doing battle with the world and the skirmishes leave me confused and sad. Unfortunately, I am not yet enlightened, so my ego still cries out to discover its place...its value. As I move through life, my ego remains fascinated by the way others witness me in the world. As I see myself reflected in others, it often seems as if the mirror is cracked and the reflection is distorted and incomplete.

A friend told me in passing one day, "When you write, you're too deep...too philosophical. Just tell people what to do!" Without warning, I found my emotions battling for control of the future into which I was about to wander. I don't take criticism well. From somewhere in my past, even helpful suggestions feel like a critique of who I am. A little voice shows up that seems to scream, "I told you that you were doing your life wrong!"

Am I doing my life wrong? There is an inner voice that wonders if it is possible to do life wrong. All we can do is be in the world...and notice. Even if what I do hurts another, life offers ways to turn the wound into a moment of reconciliation, redemption and healing.

As I reflected on the suggestion I am too philosophical, I wondered if the things I say...the things I commit to writing...are too abstract for others to turn into action. Is it possible I am in the world invisible to many because what I have to say has no impact? Do the ideological boulders I heave into the pond slip through the surface without so much as a ripple?

How is it I decide who I am in the world? How much should I listen to others? When do their exhortations have value, and when are they simply demanding I become who they want me to be...not who I am?

When I can fight off the voice of insecurity—listen instead to that voice that loves me—I can hear what is true. If I listen carefully to my heart, I can avoid being swayed by the insecurities of people who want me to be something other because who I am scares, intimidates them, or simply confuses them.

When we listen with love for self, the community names our gifts. Too often we take our gifts for granted since they seem easy, obvious and readily available to everyone. It is only by seeing who we are reflected in others that we come to know who we truly are in this world. There is a time to listen to those who love us and care about us when they say "This I see in you." Then we simply need to accept it with love and humility.

So as I reflect on the "critique" I received, I choose to listen to the voice that honors my ability to see the depth of the world. I choose to be grateful for those moments when I can ask others to see in a very different way and ask "Is it possible the world really is that way?" They may not know how to turn that new thinking into concrete action in the very next moment, but when people begin to think differently, it is simply impossible to continue to act from the old paradigm.

I am thankful for the moments I have been granted to think about who I am in the world, and yes...to sooth my fragile ego. I am in a search, in my own simple way, for the meaning of life...or at least the meaning of my life. If I give up the deep search for meaning, it feels as if something in me will die.[2]

---

[2] I first heard the phrase "something in me would die" when I had the opportunity to interview Dee Hock, CEO emeritus of Visa International. He told me that whenever he considers compromising his values, "it feels as if something in me would die."

If It Were That Easy...

If it were that easy, we would all do it, and put an end to much of human misery.

The world can be frightening for any of us, but for teens who are struggling to awaken to who they are in the world, it's especially difficult. Recently, a courageous young man led a conversation with thirty or more of his peers. He invited them to put pen to paper and anonymously suggest topics for discussion. While the ensuing conversation ranged widely, it spent some time wandering the treacherous terrain of drug addiction, depression, bullying, and the pain that often flows from failed relationships and young love.

As the teens shared the challenges they face, it became clear that elevated self-esteem and self-worth might remedy, or at least assuage, some of their misery. It is, after all, difficult to destroy, or even harm, a human who enjoys a strong sense of worth. Most of us know well the childhood aphorism, "Sticks and stones can break my bones, but names will never hurt me." But a name can hurt, maim or even kill, when hurled viciously at a human in doubt of their value.

There were several adults stung by the awareness that these wonderful young people were in pain, and lacked the personal armor to protect them against the "slings and arrows of outrageous fortune." Few of us knew how to respond other than to offer reassurances. "You have to know you are valuable," "You are all amazing," or "Don't ever doubt yourself." We utter these words with kindness and generosity, even though we know full-well that when we are beaten and battered by the world, unable to glimpse our self-worth, being told we should not turn a blind eye to our inner value is of little help. A typical private reaction to such a command might begin "If only they knew—."

While teens are particularly vulnerable to the poison arrows that can pierce their fragile self-worth, most of us find ourselves wandering the darkness sometime during our lives. I know I have been brought to my knees any number of times when I failed as a spouse, parent or friend. Few things claw at my self-worth more ferociously than the fear that I may have damaged the worth of those I love.

And yet, even in those moments we are least able to glimpse our own value, most of us can look at others and be witness to, and blessed by, theirs. Why is it we can have such clarity in discerning the value of others, and be so blind to our own? Many years ago, I was given a hint when visiting with improvisational pianist, Michael Jones. He suggested that our true gifts come to us so naturally, we believe they are nothing special. When another holds up a mirror so we can see our gifts reflected back to us, we are as likely as not to disavow their uniqueness. "Oh that! That's easy," we argue. "Anyone could do that." Michael, himself, denied his rare ability to spontaneously tease melodies from the ivories of his piano until he was more than 30. He subsequently sold several million CDs worldwide.

When I find myself wandering the darkness, certain my life is, as a friend once feared, a "throwaway line," can I find the courage to look into the world and find those willing to bow in my direction? Can I allow myself to look into the mirror they hold up and see myself as they do? Instead of immediately denying the gifts they see in me, can I take a moment to sincerely absorb their wisdom and generosity, and say "Thank you, I am honored."?

It can be very difficult, but, as I suggested as I began, if it were that easy...

Allowing You to be You

"I felt alone—on the outside looking in," Joe said as we stood at the bar.

No, that's simply not possible. I was at my 30th high school reunion talking to the former captain of the football team...the ultimate insider. He was the guy those of us 'truly' on the outside often wished we could trade places with. He was the one raising a ruckus in the library, getting all the laughs. He had all the 'right' friends.

"Roger," he continued, "I was the only one from my grade school to transfer to Catholic Central. All the rest of you arrived with friends. Do you know how alone I felt?"

There I was, at the Knights of Columbus Hall in a small town in Michigan and my world was being rearranged. Thirty-year-old thought patterns that affected who I was to become were being torn apart.

Why, I wonder, was it necessary for me to rewrite his life? Did I create him in a way that would reinforce the image I had of myself? Why was I so intimidated by who I made him to be that I was never able to inquire as to who he was? I would never have attempted such an inquiry, because the person I made him to be, would have laughed at my suggestion that he was lonely. I was certain he would have crushed me with a simple gesture that would have reinforced my self-image. I was so certain of who he was that there was no reason to even test the theory.

So now I wonder, what in my life today is real? Whose life am I rewriting as a predictable cliché, so that the quirks I implant into their life help me justify my own foibles? Who am I shoving into personality cubbyholes simply to explain who I am...or justify who I believe I am not?

Perhaps my challenge is not to be more authentic, but to put my insecurities aside long enough to allow you to be.

This was never on any of my high school exams. Perhaps it should have been.

A Time I Will Not See

> *"Children are the living messages we send to a time we will not see."*
> Neil Postman

I love Neil Postman's insight, even though it speaks so forcefully of my own mortality. There will be, in the briefest of moments, a time I will not see.

None of us will be remembered. My children, and a few of their friends perhaps, will remember me, as will the next generation, albeit with far less intensity. If I am remembered a third or fourth generation hence, it will be at most in wisps…an occasional anecdote, image or memory. Beyond that I am quite certain the human whose moniker was Roger Breisch will be long forgotten.

But Postman reminds me of a different kind of immortality. Any time humans imprint wisdom upon one another, each moves into the future carrying the messages learned from the other. Thoughts change, actions change and the future becomes something new. When we have the unique opportunity to touch the lives of children and young adults, there is the possibility some small piece of us will live into a more distant—and different—future. That thought brings tears to my eyes when a teen at Snowball, or a young caller on the suicide hotline, admits to some new thought or understanding as a result of our few moments together.

But that view puts me at the center, as progenitor of messages to the future. What if I am not?

Last summer I attended my 45th high school reunion. A classmate reproduced with pen & ink all 250 portraits from our senior yearbook—his reproduction of my portrait appears on the previous page.

The image was large, perhaps 12 by 15 inches. From the moment I saw it, I was astonished how well the young man I knew those many years ago was captured. When we returned home, I unfurled the portrait on the kitchen counter. I was struck how the eyes followed me regardless of the angle from which I tried to elude them.

Suddenly, the ink on paper came to life. As I peered with more care and a bit of compassion, it was no longer simply a sketch on the counter—the person I knew so intimately for the first 18 years of his life was staring at me. It was an unexpected moment of intimacy between two people who knew one another well, but each had somehow forgotten the other existed.

His eyes seemed to look deeper into me than any others I could recall. It was as if that young man could see me, the man he was to become, in the same way I could see him. He was able to examine the life he was to live. I could hold nothing back, since he would see every moment of joy and grace, and live into every mistake, from the minuscule to those that remain intensely painful.

For nearly a year, that young man has stared at me expectantly, and I have struggled to discern what it is he might be asking.

Then it came to me. Just as today, I show up in the lives of young people with as much authenticity as I can so they might discern a message that fits their lives, in the years when that image was first captured, there were hundreds of adults whose lives taught me something unique about what it means to be human. "Are you," that young man seems to be asking me today, "living with integrity, sincerity and love into the messages those extraordinary humans formed within us?"

Suddenly, in the world I now discern, I am the carrier rather than progenitor of messages. It is humbling to remember I am simply the medium through which their wisdom is gifted to the future. If, along the way, I add some small bit of insight to theirs, then I too will live into untold generations yet unborn. But for now, I will try, with integrity, sincerity and love, to be the living message they hoped I might be in order to ensure their lives live into the time they can no longer see.

On the Eve of an Inventure

Tomorrow begins, at least for those of us recently invited to be on staff, another Operation Snowball weekend. If we are open to it, tomorrow also begins a new world...a new future. If I am truly open, tomorrow holds the possibility of a new me.

I am prompted in these words by a book I just finished on the subject of memes. Memes are the mental, intellectual, and cultural counterparts to human genes. They are the thoughts, the ideas, the worldviews we hold and those we spread. Like the genes we pass on to our children, and generations yet unborn, memes are the ideas we implant in others that will fight for survival as they collide with alternate worldviews—conflicting ideas that simply cannot share the limited neuronal capacity of our all-too-human brains.

A phrase I once heard that brings me to tears as I contemplate my reason for existence—here at Snowball, as well as here on Earth—is "youth are the messages we send to a future we will never see." Why does it tear at my heart? Partly because it reminds me that someday, in the natural course of events, I will no longer be here for my children in their time of need...and I will not be here for the youth of Operation Snowball who so often need a kind word or hug to let them know that, in spite of their pain, they will be okay.

But I wonder if the tears come from a deeper place...from a deep sense of inadequacy. Who am I to think I am nearly wise enough to teach these beautiful young people even a small portion of what they need to know as they navigate the oft-treacherous rapids flowing toward the future. Who am I to think I have nearly the capacity to give them even a small portion of the love they ache to find in their lives. Who am I to think that I know even a smattering of the memes that will help them build a future where they can discover fulfillment and a share of happiness?

The reality is that these are actually the wrong questions. These questions put me at the center of their future. These questions hold out the possibility that I have their answers, when, in fact, I often cannot even answer the deepest questions in my own life.

So what are some better questions? A Buddhist monk once said that if we could truly see into the soul of other humans we would never get anything done...we would spend the rest of our lives bowing to one another. I believe that to be true. We have all seen it revealed through the magic that is Snowball. Often, the stories unveiled during the weekend give us a glimpse into the sacredness of the souls who sit in our midst.

So what are the right questions? Here are a few that come to mind: How can I model for these ambassadors to the future the search for self? How can I, by honestly revealing the hills and valleys of my path, help them know the path they are on is the right path, even though, for so many, their path is infinitely more difficult than mine? How can I learn to find and bow to the sacredness inside me, and by so doing, point the way to their learning of their own wholeness? How can I learn that the answers I seek are here inside my heart and that if I trust, they will reveal themselves? How can I help others discover they too already have the answers they seek?

I titled this piece "The Eve of an Inventure"—a word I borrowed from author and friend, Richard Leider. An inventure is a journey inward. An inventure is a sacred look inside my being. An inventure is a discovery of who I am, so who I truly am can manifest itself in the world.

So as we begin, I bow to each of you, my fellow travelers. I bow to your goodness…I bow to your humanity…I bow to your wisdom. And I ask for your love and support as I try to bow to myself.

Third Inquiry:
Questions Of & About Others

Do you know who you are? In my experience, many people see themselves through an opaque veil which makes it difficult to see their astonishing humanity.

Take a moment to scan the words in Figure 1 and pick four or five you might use to describe yourself[3]. Once you've done that, call to mind a specific person who knows you well, and cares about you greatly.

```
adorable    annoying  ambitious
intelligent  fun                awkward
            confident fat  friendly
disappointment        amazing        happy
          stupid           boring
   weird       caring hated         funny
         welcoming            failure cute
kind  weak         unwanted
              pretty          helpful
  unpopular  loser    worthless     lazy
   honest         creative    trash
           alone
       popular  brave  depressed   ugly
   lame        awesome   smart   ignorant
```

FIGURE 1

Rescan Figure 1 and choose 4 or 5 words they would use to describe you.

Are the two lists different? Most people with whom I have done this exercise admit theirs are—not totally different, but different in surprising ways.

No doubt you noticed there are nearly equal numbers of positive, reinforcing descriptors and negative, devaluing ones. Does your list of self-descriptors contain a few that left you in a negative light? Even if devaluing words did not make your list, did your heart skip a beat when you saw one or two because you feared they should be on your list?

How about the second list—words loved ones would choose to describe you? Is the list you chose for yourself a less positive view than the description a loved one would construct? Again, most people admit their self-description is less positive than the one they imagine from a loved one.

The question I always ask is "Why?" A typical answer is, "I know myself better than others know me."

---

[3] I compiled this list by asking a large group of teens to write down, anonymously, words they might use to describe themselves. Several suggestions, like "hungry", did not make the list!

Is that true? One young man suggested his mother's description of him would likely include the word adorable...his would not. After spending some time in conversation, I concluded that his own description would be incomplete if he rejected that word. The kindness and generosity that emanated from him clearly made him worthy of adoration!

So, how is it that our view of self can often differ greatly from the view others have of us?

The human brain is a pattern-making marvel. Since we cannot possibly take in the nearly infinite quantity of visual, auditory, emotional, olfactory and sensory information with which we are bombarded every waking moment, we notice, and place in memory, a very limited amount, and use that filtered information to construct our view of the world.

Examine Kanisza's Triangle (Figure 2) and decide if the black triangle is larger or smaller than the white one. Same size?

Actually, there are no triangles in the image Gaetano Kanizsa first created in 1955. There are six independent black shapes, but the human brain has trouble seeing them as independent because it strives to discover patterns. Your brain's pattern-making capacity "creates" two

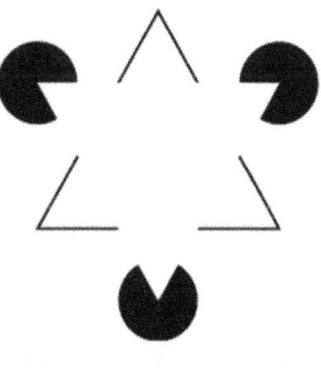

FIGURE 2

triangles. You see them, but they don't exist.[4]

So it is with our own lives. We cannot see or remember every action we took, word we uttered or thought we experienced. Instead, we choose an extremely limited number of memories and use them to create a picture of who we are. Can you be certain you are choosing fairly? Are the snippets that create the patterns of your life weighted heavily by moments of deep embarrassment, profound sadness or horrific pain? Many people, as they construct a self-image, dwell more heavily on mistakes, missteps, pain and suffering. The picture they create is of a human being defined by failure and suffering.

When loved ones tell us who they see in us, they choose differently. They focus less on our failures. Why? Imagine what people who love you would say about the mistakes you might feel define your life. They would say *exactly* what you would say to them about the failures they feel define their lives. You would remind them they are only human. "Everyone makes mistakes. Those missteps make you imminently human, not a failure." You would likely be saddened they are so very hard on themselves for their imperfect, but understandable, humanity.

When constructing an image of self, if we were to rely less on our memories of times we let ourselves down, might we witness a human we can love? Is it, perhaps, time to let go of some of the stories we feel define us?

---

[4] Visual artists will sometimes argue this point.

When our hearts break

It's up to us. We can spend our lives cultivating our resentments and cravings or we can explore the path of the warrior—nurturing open-mindedness and courage.[5]

The American Buddhist nun Pema Chödrön reminds me there is an important difference between letting go of the story, and holding on to, and learning from, the feelings and emotions that arise from the experience. The sorrow, joy, anxiety, anger, pain and other emotions we feel, are powerful teachers if we are willing to explore them without remaining defined by the story through which they emerged. These moments help us to understand, and love, all other beings—even those who have hurt us.

From the Hasidic tradition comes a tale. A disciple asks the rebbe: "Why does Torah tell us to place these words upon our hearts? Why does it not tell us to place these holy words *in* our hearts?" The rebbe answers: "It is because as we are, our hearts are closed, and we cannot place the holy words in our hearts. So we place them on top of our hearts. And there they stay until, one day, the heart breaks and the words fall in."

How many of us honor those moments when our hearts break and allow the holy words to fall in? When our heart breaks, we can allow it to be filled with a new, deeper understanding of what it means to be human. We gain empathy, learn greater generosity and increase our ability to love. Our heart grows. In those moments, if we sit with

---

[5] The Places That Scare You: A Guide to Fearlessness in Difficult Times, Pema Chödrön. ©2001, Shambhala Publications, Inc., page 37

our brokenness, there is a still-point of holiness and wisdom we can live into the world.

What might be different about this moment, the next moment and the infinity of moments beyond, if we could recall the sacred wisdom we have been bequeathed, and live it into the world? How would the future be different if we could better understand the limitations of our thoughts and words, learn to appreciate the infinite, and recapture the wonder and innocence we may have lost?

The essays in the Third Inquiry recall times I realized how easily people do violence to themselves, when what they need is love, kindness and generosity.

In "Nothing Stunning...Really?" I relate the wisdom of improvisational pianist, Michael Jones. I had the good fortune to spend time with him many years ago. He reminded me the gifts we hold most deeply within are such an integral part of who we are they are often invisible to us. We find them by asking the truth-tellers in our lives to help us see that to which we are blind, but then we need to find the courage to see.

"Sex in a Fishbowl" was an intervention we use with teens at Snowball. It gives them a safe venue, and anonymity, so they can ask questions about relationships with the opposite sex. I discovered, however, there are still many questions about sense of self—and my relationship with myself—that are too difficult for even this safe place.

A videogame was the inspiration for "The Layers of Who We Are Not." Life gives us many moments to discover who we are...and many moments that conceal us. When we meet life head on, we are presented with many opportunities to put aside aspects of self that no longer fit, and open ourselves to new understandings. Often, we face pain and heartache so overwhelming that all we want is to do is retreat from life. If, instead, if we are open to their lessons, those moments can lead us back into the world with greater wisdom, compassion and generosity.

At an Operation Snowball weekend retreat, the teens asked me to speak to our own lovability. "Help us understand that we are lovable," they asked. As I tried to assemble my thoughts it became clear I could not ask them to love themselves until I first came to love myself. "Listen and Believe" tells of the journey to find my own lovability, prior to speaking of theirs.

In "Majesty and Radiance" I recall how the human brain is incapable of taking in everything it encounters, so it filters information by necessity. As a result, we often look back upon the events of our lives and focus only on those that do not serve us. When we do, we find ourselves to be worth less than the majesty and radiance that existence itself bestows.

"Acknowledging with Grace, Gratitude and Humility" recounts the touching relationship between a young man and his father. When others tell us of the beauty and magnificence they see in us, are we willing to take it in, or does our embarrassment in the moment leave the impression we question the veracity or generosity of those who come offering such a gift? How might we show our deep respect for the truth-tellers in our lives by summoning the courage to accept those moments with grace, gratitude and humility?

Finally, "How Are You Doing" asks you to examine the way in which you act in the world. Can actions based on anxiety, anger, greed and frustration, be approached, instead, with generosity, care, love and concern?

Nothing Stunning...Really?

If I asked, would you tell me of your gifts—the unique, stunning aspects of your humanity and journey that make you like no other human ever born? Even if you were able, would you be willing? Or would you, like so many, feel anxious and find yourself filled with unknowing and confusion? Even worse, would you feel compelled to say there is nothing stunning about you?

A friend, Michael Jones, is an exceptional improvisational pianist and elder—one who passes along the stories, values and wisdom of the tribe. When Michael's fingertips fall upon a keyboard, he and the piano become one, and glorious melodies emerge from them unbidden.

Michael bared his soul to me in 1998 when we recorded, and subsequently published, a marvelous interview. We sat next to his magnificent Bosendorfer grand piano as he spoke of his journey, and how his inner flame was nearly extinguished when he was very young. I asked how such a gift could be lost. "It came in bringing a piece of my music to a piano lesson. My teacher, a very kindly person, expressed relatively little real interest. The real work was to play the masters. This creation of mine wasn't going to measure up. I felt embarrassed and self-conscious."

Michael's journey was altered many years later when an elderly stranger caught him playing what appeared to be a secluded piano in a quiet hotel lobby. When Michael tried to disavow the splendor and uniqueness of his musical gifts, this unexpected guide asked him *"Who is going to play your music if you don't play it yourself?"*

Michael has since shared his music on more than a dozen CDs with millions sold around the world. "To think," Michael confided in me, "there was that much music I was carrying inside and had no sense was there. We have no perception of what is waiting to be made manifest."

What would Michael say to that elderly gentleman today? "I would thank all those people who—in that moment of perception and courage—have been able to see into the essence of the other and give it voice. That's how we can best serve one another…to see in the other what they cannot see in themselves."

Michael went on to say, "We don't get help in our culture to understand what it means to belong to ourselves and the world. There are many cultures where musicians would never think of playing anybody else's music! In the West we play almost exclusively other people's music—as a metaphor, but also literally. We feel embarrassed to bring something that is our own."

We see the gifts that come to us most naturally as nothing special. "That's easy," we say to ourselves and the world, "anyone could do *that*!"

"More people are becoming aware there is deeper music in their life…sensing the call to let their lives and work be a reflection of that music," Michael suggested. "The challenge is, we have to put aside the script…the musical score. When that gentleman spoke to me, I felt absolute clarity in terms of what was significant in my life, *but I was totally lost in terms of what to do with it.* Being lost is part of the journey. There is something we need to access within ourselves that only arises when we feel lost, confused or uncertain. There is the tradition that says, if you can see the path clearly laid in front of you, chances are you've stumbled onto someone else's path!"

As I have struggled to discern my path in this world, I have asked those who know me and care for me to help me see what I cannot see in myself. Then, when a friend leans in close and points me in the direction of my "music," I struggle to quiet the voice that screams in dissent, *"Anyone could do that!"*

So, when you find yourself lost, confused and uncertain, take comfort in knowing that this just may be your rightful path for now. Then consider seeking out guides who know and love you. Listen, and seek the courage to believe what they tell you. Finally, thank them for their willingness to see into the essence of the other and give it voice.

Listen and Believe

There is a Buddhist tale about parents who asked a local monk to teach their child to live free of anger and hatred. "Of course," replied the monk. "Bring your child back in two years." Two years later they returned and instruction commenced. Confused, they asked why the teachings had to wait. "Because," the monk replied, "First, I had to learn to live free of anger and hatred."

At Operation Snowball, the teen program for which I volunteer, we use the acronym IALAC: I Am Lovable And Capable. About a month before our spring retreat the teen directors asked me to speak about IALAC for the 130 or more teens who would attend. The moment they asked, I recalled the Buddhist story and my heart skipped a beat. "I must first come to believe I am lovable," I thought "and I don't have two years to discern the truth."

Everyone has moments in which the reflection they witness in the mirror of life is of a person they find difficult to love. I recall many failures as a parent, when ego and insecurity prevented me from being the kind, gentle and wise guide I hoped to be for my children; failures as a husband, when attending to *my* agenda left my wife feeling abandoned and lonely; failures in my career, where I anticipated becoming a captain of industry...forty years later my resume is a train-wreck by most traditional measures.

Father, Husband, Provider. If these roles define a man's life, and you feel you have failed, it can be challenging to look in the mirror and perceive a person who is lovable.

As the weeks slipped by, I struggled to find the lens through which I could see myself as unconditionally lovable. And because teens are still apprentices at life, their mistakes, hurts and scars can seem crushingly painful, and leave them feeling hopelessly unloved and unlovable. If I struggle to see myself as unconditionally lovable, how could I provide them a lens of lovability through which they could perceive themselves?

At some moment the path opened. The teens themselves are, and have been for ten years, the lens through which I can see myself as lovable. I have hundreds of handwritten notes—words that leave me humbled and in tears—in which teens have held up unblemished mirrors to help me see what they see. Their view can be a more genuine reflection than mine because, in my mirror, the brutal voice of failure vies for dominance over the quiet, often shy and cautious voice that knows I am lovable.

So when the time came to speak, after I described the critical self-reflection to which I am often witness, I asked, by show of hands, how many have seen something in me that is lovable. The response, in all humility, brought me to my knees. "What if," I suggested, "I step out of my body, leave Roger here in front, and come sit amongst you." I made a gesture of stepping out of my own body, and I sat down in their midst.

As I sat, surrounded by these loving young truth-tellers, looking up at the virtual person I left standing before us, it became easier to see a man who—in spite of his failures, missteps and scars—cares deeply and tries mightily. Suddenly I was able to glimpse a man who is lovable.

So I returned to the question that began our time together: Are we, each of us, lovable and capable of love?

"Of that," I said "there is no doubt. From the moment you were conceived, in every moment since, and in each moment into the future, you are infinitely lovable and capable of love." "It is," I continued, "fundamentally the wrong question. The real question is, 'Are you willing to find the courage to listen and believe?'"

When life leaves us questioning our worth—leaves us feeling hopeless—it is helpful to find a truth-teller…someone who loves us and will recount honestly what they see in us. All that remains is to look, with an open heart, into the reflection they so generously offer, silence the voice of denial, and summon the courage to listen and believe.

Sex in a Fishbowl[6]

At Operation Snowball, the teens call the exercise "Sex in a Fishbowl," but it's not some weird, erotic game. They divide the room sending males to one side with females facing them from the other. Everyone scribbles questions they would like their counterparts of the opposite sex to answer, and places them into a fishbowl to be withdrawn randomly and anonymously.

Anxiety fills the room as the questions emerge, and becomes especially ubiquitous when they migrate from the mundane to those that swirl around relationships and how we can test them for validity and legitimacy. "How do you know when a girl likes you?" "How do you tell the guy you are dating that you like them?" These are among the questions that cause the most squirming...and elicit the most embarrassed answers. On the surface, simple questions in search of straightforward answers.

But, I wonder, are the answers we seek actually in search of far deeper questions? Are the unasked questions, those lurking in background, not about how acceptance bounces from one to another, but how acceptance resounds within me? Could it be that the real questions are "Do I like and value myself, and how do I know?"

---

[6] I chuckle at the title of this essay. No other post on my website draws as many views as this. I can only imagine the disappointment faced by many who may be seeking some "weird, exotic" tantric description. At Snowball we have changed the name of this exercise to "Middle School Dance" to capture the anxiety and discomfort of adolescence.

Perhaps I am unusual, but, for most of my life, and certainly as I raced through puberty, I have been in search of a self worthy of my respect. Can I tease from my being a self deserving of the resources it consumes, a self that leaves behind greater value than it finds, and most frighteningly, a self that someone might love? To this very day, it is possible, often easy, for me to fall into a place of deep questioning of self-worth and value…and let's not even get into questions of lovability.

The need to be loved and valued is, I believe, deeply rooted in the human psyche. I know many people who are responsible for meaningful change in the human condition and they still question the meaning of their lives. One dear friend I grew to love and admire for her lifetime of work said, as she approached the end of her time on Earth, "I don't want my life to have been a throwaway line." Another of my teachers reflected that, "When you ask people about their gifts and you get platitudes…ask about their faults and you get poetry!"

Each of us has gifts and an inner beauty; each of us has value and is lovable. But those qualities can be difficult to see in good times. In our darker moments, they can become impossible to touch. Or feel.

In the Zen Buddhist tradition there are cautions against this kind of attachment to "self." The Buddha suggested that the root of all suffering is attachment. Nirvana is that place where we free ourselves from wishes that we, and the world around us, could be different. Freedom is the complete acceptance of what is. But I wonder if the path to Nirvana requires us to traverse the valley of doubt. Could it be that it is only after we discover a valuable self that we can finally let it go and end the search?

Human relationships are complex, difficult and often break our hearts; but if they were otherwise—easy to understand and incapable of touching our hearts—of what value would they be? They are the gateways into the valley of doubt and self-questioning.

So, as you ask me about the validity of our relationship—whether I like you and you like me—I ask for your understanding if I squirm. To entertain those questions is to invite you into a deeply personal, and sometimes frightening, introspective dialogue. The answers to those seemingly simple questions are waiting for me to answer the larger question of how much I care for myself—questions that emerged long before a fishbowl appeared in the middle of the room. And those deeper answers are nearly sixty years in the making.

The Layers of Who We Are Not

I recall a video game, Tetrisphere, which is a variation of Tetris. In the game the player confronts a sphere covered by three-dimensional shapes. The game provides the player with a series of objects similar in shape to those covering the sphere. When you match a piece with one on the outermost layer of the sphere, it disappears and reveals a small portion of a level nearer the sphere's core. The object is to eliminate enough pieces to open the core and release a friendly little robot.

One challenging aspect of the game is the sphere grows with time, making it more difficult for the player to reach the core before time runs out.

From the beginning, Tetrisphere struck me as a powerful metaphor for life. We are continually given experiences of life in the form of challenges, joys, suffering, love and confusion. Each piece of life—a different size, shape and color—is an invitation to fit it into our knowing, or unknowing. When we live these experiences with authenticity and vulnerability, the wisdom we gain tears away a small piece of who we may have thought we were to expose a slightly deeper level of our true selves. The goal of life, perhaps, is to tear away enough layers to release into the world the essence of who we are.

If, on the other hand, we allow experiences, especially those that are painful and difficult, to add to the layers that separate us from the core of who we are, it becomes more difficult to discover who we were meant to be.

A call came from a young man who had difficulty seeing his self-worth. He made a decision that had unpleasant consequences for those he loved. Because of the pain he caused, he felt he was a horrible, selfish person—new layers making it more difficult to see himself for who he truly is.

Even "poor" decisions are usually made in the best way we know at the moment of choice. I asked, early in the conversation, if that was true for him. "No!" he insisted. "I knew better...I should never have made that choice." He told me his heart felt dirty, sullen and hidden.

In the midst of the call, I wondered silently "Why do we find it so difficult to offer ourselves the generosity and understanding we offer others?" As our relationship developed I began to grasp the overpowering anxiety pervading his life at the time of his fateful decision. It was so strong it clouded his view of life and pointed him to the decision he eventually made. When I asked him about his panic and apprehension, he reluctantly admitted he did, indeed, feel a loss of control over his life. So I asked, "If you were to show yourself the kindness you would show another, would you be willing to admit you are indeed a good and kind person, who, in a moment of confusion, made a choice you now reject?" There was a moment of silence after which he said quietly, "Maybe so." He paused for a moment longer, and then he asked, "Do you think the pain I am feeling is my heart trying to find its way back into the world?"

Even as I write these words, tears well up. I could do nothing in the moments that followed but be in awe of the profundity of his insight. It was one more of life's experience pointing him to the magnificence of who he is behind the layers of who he is not.

Majesty and Radiance

Funny, how the cost of a ball can lead me to thoughts of the value of life itself.

Several recent books reflect upon the human brain and the vast amount of sensory data with which it is barraged. Even at this moment, there is nearly infinite visual, auditory, olfactory, savory and corporeal information bombarding you, and you will absorb, consciously and subconsciously, a minuscule percent. What fascinates me is how the mind can take in—by the nature in which you choose to notice—data that are disparate, incongruent, and misleading, and create what we believe is a coherent picture of the world. How often are the decisions we make, and the conclusions we draw, based on truly accurate representations of the world?

As a simple example, if I tell you that, together, a bat and ball cost $1.10, and that the bat costs a dollar more than the ball, can you tell me the cost of the ball? 10¢? Excellent! I'll sell it to you for 10¢ because it cost half that. If the ball cost 10¢, the bat costs a dollar, which is only 90¢ more than the ball.

Suppose I asked you the average height of the redwoods of California. If I prefaced my request by suggesting they are shorter than 1200 feet tall, your estimate would likely be larger than if I began by telling you they are taller than 150 feet. In replicated experiments, the human brain gets "anchored" to the number first suggested and moves from there; down a small distance from 1200 feet or up some from 150, suggesting answers that are closer to the anchor than to reality.

Did you know that most people, including you perhaps, turn right as they enter stores?[7] It is no coincidence the fruits and vegetables are typically the first thing you encounter. Placing healthy items in your cart as you begin your shopping allows you to feel slightly less guilty when you tuck candy and less healthy food in beside it. School cafeterias can change youthful diets simply by the placement of the menu choices.

A fascinating series of experiments that test for a person's feelings of generosity indicate that the presence of money has a negative impact. When currency is displayed so the subject can see it, *even if it has nothing to do with the experiment*, people become less generous in the ensuing moments. It's true, even if we are not sure why.

All this suggests that whenever we make a decision, or draw a conclusion about the world, we should remember that our view is built on a foundation of limited, disparate information. The human mind will use that incomplete, narrow and inadequate evidence in fickle and often misleading ways.

Not long ago I spoke with a woman who, the evening before, fell victim to a frail part of her humanity. She slipped into a very human pattern and subsequently said angry, hurtful things to her boyfriend. She knows him to be kind and loving; not at all deserving of the things she said. As a result, she felt herself to be malicious and evil, and was tearfully questioning her value as a human being.

---

[7] I am not certain if this is true only in countries that drive on the right side of the road.

The two of us talked about what it means to be human; that everyone fails to live up to their ideals of perfection from time to time. Our brief conversation allowed us to build a relationship based on acceptance of our humanity, rather than judgment of occasional failure. When I asked her to peer more deeply into her world and see if she might find even a small bit of goodness and value, she paused and quietly admitted, "Maybe...just a little." "Is it possible the goodness within is far larger than you are able to see in this moment, and the angry, worthless parts are much smaller?" She paused again a bit longer this time and said "Yes, I think so." Soon, she was eager to apologize to her boyfriend, work diligently to avoid future failures, knowing full well that, being human nearly assures she will.

It matters little if we peer into the world, absorb limited, incongruent data, and conclude incorrectly that a ball is worth 10¢. But if we gaze into the world and find ourselves to be worth less than the majesty and radiance that existence itself bestows, is it time to reach out and find someone who can hold up a mirror that better reflects the beauty inherent in life?

Acknowledging with Grace, Gratitude and Humility

His smile is huge and welcoming, and he has a personality to match. He admitted he is uncomfortable with hugs and tears, but on an Operation Snowball weekend, taking off the masks we wear to protect ourselves, and being vulnerable, is an invaluable part of the experience.

In spite of the tough veneer, there was a moment the façade unexpectedly slipped. As he spoke innocently of his family, he began to tell us of his birth-father—his parents had divorced many years earlier. "My Dad is my hero," he began innocently enough, but as he continued his eyes welled up and he tried desperately to hold back the tears. "As a young man, he was in a gang—it's part of the reason he and my mother split. But, about the time I was born, he straightened out his life. He works harder than anyone I know. I love him *so* much." With that, he wiped away the tears that made their way down his face.

"Have you ever told him what you just told us?" I asked. "I've tried," he said. "It's really hard, but sometimes as I'm leaving, I'll turn and tell him I love him." "No," I pressed, "Have you ever looked him square in the eye and said 'Dad, you are my hero. I love you more than I can even say.'" He stared at the floor and admitted he had not.

Why, when we see magnificence in another, especially one we love, do we frequently find it difficult to acknowledge? Perhaps it's because a moment of affirmation requires vulnerability from both giver and receiver. When I am honored by another, it can trigger memories of the frailties I often believe define me. I can become embarrassed and confused in the face of sincere, caring affirmation and deflect the recognition…and in my inelegance, embarrass the person who only wants me to see something wonderful within.

What if, in an unexpectedly touching moment with his son, a formerly tough gang member, in confusion and embarrassment, blurted, "Don't be silly, I'm not that great!" All the son might hear from the man he adores is the crushing implication he is silly.

Later that weekend, I sought out that young man. "At the risk of pushing too hard and being a pain in your backside, may I tell you a story?" "Sure," he said with a curious smile.

"My daughter invited me to join her on a Snowball weekend when she was a sophomore in high school. Snowball changed my life and I am grateful beyond measure. At her last event as a senior, I pulled her aside one last time to tell her how thankful I was she invited me on this journey we shared. She looked me in the eye and said 'Dad, I truly believe the reason I got involved was to bring you here. You are my gift to Snowball.' I was stunned."

"That was more than six years ago," I continued, "yet, I remember that moment as if it was yesterday. I will take those words with me to my grave. If you tell your father how much you love and admire him, don't be deterred if his initial reaction is tainted by confusion and embarrassment. In the end, I am certain he will, as well, carry your words with him until the day he dies."

At the end of the weekend, that "tough" young man left a note for me in which he said I was the sweetest man on Earth and that he loved me. And now, despite my own embarrassment, tears are having their way with me.

I am left with two questions. Will I remember to tell others more frequently of the joy their presence infuses into my in my life? Will I, even more diligently, when told of the joy others discover as a result of my presence in their life, acknowledge their affirmation with grace, gratitude and humility?

How Are You Doing?

How are you doing? But before you answer, think carefully...there might be more at stake than you think.

I might be wrong, but there is a good chance your immediate response would have been to a question other than the one I intended. If you are like most people, you were tempted to say something like "Fine, thanks," "Couldn't be better," "Not so great," or perhaps "Life has been a struggle, but I'll make it through." Those are answers to the inquiry "How are you?" What I asked is "How are you doing?"...as in "In what manner are you completing the task in front of you at this moment?" Recently, I have begun to wonder if the manner in which I approach the activities of my life is just as important, or perhaps far more important, than the activities themselves. I have been reflecting on my "to be" list as actively as my "to do" list.

Having watched some of the Games of the XXX Olympiad, athletes know attitude is critical when translating mental desire into physical results. On a golf course, if I pull a driver from my bag and approach the ball with confidence, I am far more likely to hit a solid drive than if I approach with the belief that hitting a microscopic white orb with a small mallet at the far end of a very long graphite shaft is simply impossible. (You now know why I haven't played golf in twenty years!) I was on my bicycle recently when I came upon a very narrow path, perhaps fifty feet in length, bounded on both sides by a high railing. While I never have trouble keeping my bike steady in the open, once bounded by the railing, fear welled up and made the first 30 feet a difficult and treacherous escapade. Once I neared the end of the challenge, my confidence returned and the final 15 feet were easy to negotiate.

My attitude toward day-to-day activities has an impact far beyond how my brain's neuronal impulses might ease or challenge the movements of my muscles. If I am filled with animosity as I wend my way through my daily toils, will I create different outcomes than if I am joyful and filled with gratitude? Are interactions with others, especially my family, more fruitful if I begin by remembering how much I love them, rather than entering a conversation angry over a perceived lack of respect or difference of opinion? When I begin my interactions by reminding myself to focus on their wholeness rather than mine, is life far more generative? There is a reason why we say "if you're angry, count to ten before you speak."

Edward Lorenz was a meteorologist, who, in 1969, coined the term *Butterfly Effect*, when he discovered that infinitesimally small changes in initial conditions can radically change the course of weather over time and distance. It is said that a butterfly flapping its wings in one part of the world, by changing initial weather conditions ever so slightly, can cause a tornado, hurricane or tsunami weeks or months later halfway around the globe.

The Butterfly Effect applies to far more than insects and inclement weather. Any time we change initial conditions, the course of human history is altered. And while it is difficult to imagine that some distant, future international conflict may erupt because of the attitude with which I approach a golf ball, it is not difficult to see how a careless, angry comment from a parent to a child can change the course of their lives. I know…I hear from callers on the suicide hotline how tsunamis of painful emotion have erupted because of thoughtless or angry comments from important role models many years earlier.

So, I'll ask again. How are you doing? How are you approaching what you are doing in this moment, or in the very next? If you are anxious, angry, greedy or frustrated could you stop for just a moment, take a deep breath and instead approach the next moment with more generosity, care, love and concern?

It just might be that the future of humanity hangs in the balance.

*Fourth Inquiry:
How Might We Live*

Cook Ting was cutting up an ox for Lord Wen-hui. At every touch of his hand, every heave of his shoulder, every move of his feet, every thrust of his knee —zip! zoop! He slithered the knife along with a zing, and all was in perfect rhythm, as though he were performing the dance of the Mulberry Grove or keeping time to the Ching-shou music.

"Ah, this is marvelous!" said Lord Wen-hui. "Imagine skill reaching such heights!"

Cook Ting laid down his knife and replied, "What I care about is the Way, which goes beyond skill. When I first began cutting up oxen, all I could see was the ox itself. After three years I no longer saw the whole ox. And now—now I go at it by spirit and don't look with my eyes. Perception and understanding have come to a stop and spirit moves where it wants. I go along with the natural makeup, strike in the big hollows, guide the knife through the big openings, and following things as they are. So I never touch the smallest ligament or tendon, much less a main joint.

"A good cook changes his knife once a year—because he cuts. A mediocre cook changes his knife once a month—because he hacks. I've had this knife of mine for nineteen years and I've cut up thousands of oxen with it, and yet the blade is as good as though it had just come from the grindstone. There are spaces between the joints, and the blade of the knife has really no thickness. If you insert what has no thickness into such spaces, then there's plenty of room—more than enough for the blade to play about it. That's why after nineteen years the blade of my knife is still as good as when it first came from the grindstone.

"However, whenever I come to a complicated place, I size up the difficulties, tell myself to watch out and be careful, keep my eyes on what I'm doing, work very slowly, and move the knife with the greatest subtlety, until—flop!—

the whole thing comes apart like a clod of earth crumbling to the ground. I stand there holding the knife and look all around me, completely satisfied and reluctant to move on, and then I wipe off the knife and put it away."

"Excellent!" said Lord Wen-hui. "I have heard the words of Cook Ting and learned how to care for life!"[8]

How often does life feel like an effortless dance performed in perfect rhythm? I wonder if our way of living—trying to make the world conform to our wishes and desires—is more reminiscent of the mediocre cook who must sharpen his knife every month because he hacks at bones. Is plundering through life based on our own agenda inelegant and destructive? Is it possible to live another way? If we come to know ourselves intimately, might we become like the knife that has no thickness, more aware of the spaces in which we can move and play around? Might a life based on subtle movement leave us completely satisfied, rather than frustrated by collisions with obstacles that foil our plans?

Many years ago, in the midst of a discussion of resolutions for the new year, a friend said he intended to pay more attention to invitations. Paying attention to invitations has altered the course of my life.

When I spoke to the Board of Directors at Suicide Prevention Services (now SPS America) in 2003, they invited me to enroll in their training to answer calls on the hotline. In return, they asked for a one-year, 250-hour commitment. 14 years and more than 3000 hours later, I

---

[8] Chuang Tzu: The Basic Writings. Translated by Burton Watson, 1964

am still there. The wisdom that permeates my life, generously offered by those suffering unimaginable pain and heartache infuses these pages.

Eleven years ago, my daughter extended an invitation for me to join her as an adult participant on an Operation Snowball weekend with 150 teens. I recall feeling old, out-of-touch and out of place. Yet, in the ensuing years, the teens have, by opening their hearts, held up a mirror that enables me to see something inside to which I had been blind. I have hundreds of notes from these young wisdom-keepers that ask me to witness the humanity they see within and cease my denial. Their stories and wisdom are an essential part of my life.

In 2004, the Executive Director of the local Chamber of Commerce, when she discovered I was in search of a new direction, told me she was resigning and invited me to submit my resume to the board. My wanderings through the lives and businesses of hundreds of members, gave me ample opportunity to reflect on the nature of our work, and the careers we choose to animate our lives. The monthly newsletter was a frequent vessel for me to assemble thoughts about who we are in the context of our work.

In hundreds of other small ways as well, I have accepted invitations, and pushed aside personal plans and goals…schemes I might have been certain would alter the world in more dramatic ways. But the invitations permitted me to discover essential pieces of who I am and become "a knife with no thickness." Only then am I able to *"keep my eyes on what I'm doing, work very slowly, and move the knife with the greatest subtlety."*

What if a life carefully planned—a life defined and bounded by goals, deadlines, plans and to-do lists—robs us of the deepest wisdom the Universe has to offer? Is it possible that focusing on *my* agenda leaves me deaf to that which I am supposed to hear? I have heard it said far too many times that people who have plans and goals are more successful than those who fail to plan. But what is success? I might have more money had I followed my plans rather than the invitations that caused me to push plans aside, but I would never have been touched by the teens at Operation Snowball. I might have newer cars and furniture, but never heard the voices crying for solace, consolation and affirmation. I might have traveled to the far corners of the globe, but not have traversed the depths with those considering an end to their lives.

The right choices? I will never know. But of this I am certain: I simply cannot imagine abandoning the wisdom that has flowed from the many summonses I have answered.

The essays in this Fourth Inquiry were written with the tone and timbre that emerges when I imagine lives animated by invitations.

I begin with "Godspeed on My Journey," which I wrote just after leaving my last full-time position as head of the Chamber. Leaving that job gave me more freedom to ponder the imponderable. It was in the remarks I offered the final night of my tenure that I first wondered "have we learned to ask questions that truly matter?" Now, I return, perhaps for the final time, to a life defined by invitations.

In "Feather on a Breeze" I wonder how we might live if we understood the critical, overpowering role of the truly unexpected. I have been deeply moved by Nassim Nicholas Taleb who wrote the profound volume, *The Black Swan*. Taleb recounts how the unusual, the unexpected, the unplanned journeys are the *real* descriptors of life. Yet, we still want to believe life can be carefully planned and executed. How many find that, as Allen Saunders first said in 1957, "Life is what happens to us while we are making other plans."[9] I wonder how we should instruct children about life if we admit that, as John Steinbeck said in *Of Mice and Men*, "The best-laid plans of mice and men / Go oft awry." Not only do they "go oft awry," it is when they do that life becomes interesting and wisdom is there for the taking.

"Surrender…It's not for the Faint of Heart" came to me after watching the beautiful harmony that emerged as a young friend and piano melded into one. Much like when I am in the presence of Michael Jones' beautiful improvisations, it seemed unclear if pianist is playing the piano, or if the piano is enticing pianist to do its bidding. Is it possible to live a life in which we surrender to a call, and be uncertain if we are living life, or if life is being lived through us?

Rubrics, guidelines, aphorisms and rules can play an important role in helping us negotiate the oft-confusing world. But are there times when we must jettison those that bound our lives and prevent us from soaring? "Eroding the Riverbanks of Life" asks how we might know when to jettison that which imprisons us. Too often, we live lives based on stories of who we might have been, but that now prevent us from discovering who we were meant to become.

"The River of Life" suggests that life's fragile, impermanent nature might prevent us from seeing its beauty and splendor. Our lives are far different when

---

[9] The lyrics of John Lennon's "Beautiful Boy (Darling Boy)" contain the quote "Life is what happens to you while you're busy making other plans." However, the expression of this sentiment can be traced back to a 1957 Reader's Digest article, which attributes it to Allen Saunders.

viewed from a distance, much like a river when viewed from above; we are mesmerized and delighted—even though unpredictable rapids, when viewed up close, fill us with fear and terror. How should we live through our moments of terror, and remember they are part of a magnificent whole?

Can we fully accept who we are, warts and all? "On Being Fully Human," asks if our moments of inhumanity need to be acknowledged with grace and loving kindness, because they are an integral part of who we are. If each person could become the perfect beings they wish they were, might the world fail to gain the wisdom imparted to us by those who are imperfect? Might our impact on the world as perfect beings actually be less?

If our impact seems negligible during our lifetime, it's easy to feel as if our life had little meaning. In "A Message 500 Years in the Making," after witnessing the great cathedrals of Europe, I question that. The stone masons of the Middle Ages labored their entire lives with little progress to show for their efforts. Are we doing anything with our lives, the impact of which will not be visible for ten generations hence? Am I helping create anything with my life that will leave future generations, even those hundreds of years from now, in awe? Is my being far more important than my doing?

In "Kicking and Screaming" I wonder if, as I age, I will become an elder, or merely older. It is astounding to me that if you change a single letter, we refer to living fully into the final years of our lives as opposed to waiting for death to overtake us. As I age, am I willing to remain "in the question"? Will I be a life-long learner until the day I die?

Finally, "Regret at the End of Life" tells the story of a deeply spiritual ICU nurse who came to a few of our

Socrates Cafés. She stopped us short one evening with her question about the end of life. When I come to the end of mine, will I die with regret, or will my life have been enough? How must I live each day so that if tomorrow is my last, today will have been enough?

Godspeed on My Journey

Years ago, after having experienced a major life-changing event, Ram Das wrote a book entitled *Still Here*. Despite having left the Chamber of Commerce, I am still here in *Neighbors of Batavia* magazine[10]. The publishers graciously asked me to continue. Showing up in this place, authentically and emotionally, has become an integral part of my life, and I am profoundly grateful for this sanctuary.

My decision to leave the Chamber arrived unexpectedly, but the clarity with which I reached that crossroad was undeniable. I simply could no longer remain the community's chief spokesperson for business. In leaving, one of the first questions I face is, "So, what's next?" The fact that I don't know surprises many. Why leave a position, without an alternate landing pad on my flight plan? I'm not sure.

From the start, I was the most unlikely of Chamber executives. Truth be known, I don't care about the measures of success typically saddled upon such a position. Did we, in 10 years, brighten the economic environment? Did we sell more products or make more money? Are there more businesses and fewer empty store fronts? These would be measures of success for the traditional economic development professional, but in ten years, I never knew, nor did I care about, the answers to

---

[10] The publication to which I referred in the Introduction.

such inquiries. Centuries hence, it will not have mattered that we sold one more trinket, or put one more dollar into the bank.

What will matter to our progeny hundreds of years in the future? I don't know that either, but here are some thoughts...

Are we better human beings today than we were yesterday? Do we care more...love more...discern more...respect more? Are we wiser and more insightful? Do we act with honesty, integrity and authenticity? Have we learned to ask questions that truly matter? Have we found our rightful place here in this place? I don't know if we have made progress on these measures of our humanness, but of these I care deeply. In my ten years as head of the Chamber, I was always far more concerned about the business of people's lives than I was about the lives of their businesses.

The human species, as well, faces many crossroads. In my heart-of-hearts I believe we are staring over a precipice. As we move into the future it is not what we do...it is who we are that will determine if we fall precipitously from the heights, or take flight into a humane future in which we will come to discover prosperity that is stunning in its simplicity, yet beneficent beyond our imagination. It is to that quest to which I hope to turn my attention. What will be the manner and mode of my journey? Of that I am uncertain.

In the journey of life, we face unexpected crossroads. They can be a time of fear and confusion...when prosperity seems elusive and uncertain. Nevertheless, we sometimes need to leap, build our wings on the way down and trust that prosperity is abundant if we are willing to recognize it.

The subtitle of Ram Das' book is *Embracing Aging, Changing, and Dying*. While I am thankful for my continued good health, I am aging and changing. More decades are behind me than ahead. But perhaps, if I pay attention and live with ever more honesty, integrity and authenticity, I can discover my vocation and an even more prosperous life on the path ahead than the one I have already traversed.

Over the years, I ended many Chamber events by wishing those in attendance "Godspeed on your journey," without knowing its origins and meaning. The word Godspeed comes from the Middle English phrase *God spede*…"May God prosper you." For perhaps the very first time, with humility and gratitude, I am wishing myself Godspeed on my journey…and I invite you to do the same for yourself.

Feather on the Breeze

If I close my eyes, even momentarily, I can return to any number of wanderings through the woods and re-witness a bird's feather or wispy seed float past, gently buffeted by the breeze. And, as gentle as that journey might appear, the feather has no control over the direction of its travels or its destination. In the case of a seed, the future of its species might actually be transformed by this journey over which it has no control.

Jake, a wonderful friend and English teacher, used the phrase "feather on the wind," to describe life in a note he recently floated into my life. As I have thought about how to live life in the face of Black Swans—the highly improbable, impactful events described by Nassim Nicholas Taleb in his book by the same name—feather on the wind becomes a wonderful metaphor. And yet (pardon the pun), it flies in the face of much conventional wisdom. In a search of the web, the first blogger I discovered compared a feather-on-the-wind-life with one lived largely on a couch with a beer in hand and TV in view. The author spoke of the horrors of allowing the winds of life to determine where we and our seeds are planted. "Take control of your life," this author demanded as millions of his pixels splashed across my screen. Is it just me, or is the image of a feather gently following the breeze juxtaposed with a couch potato and a beer just too difficult to fathom?

What if all we have are swans? What if highly improbable, impactful events really do define my life? How might I see swans as the winds—be they gentle or vicious—

upon which my life's path is hewn? If my most carefully refined plans will ultimately collide with—and be demolished by—the unpredictable, what is the role of planning?

Don't misunderstand, I know planning is necessary and useful. I just wonder if we too often miss the mystery of life—the "road less traveled." Our lives are made up of both mystery and mastery. If we are slaves to mastering life through planning, do we risk missing the mystery...what the pianist Michael Jones once called "the path the heart loves to wander."

I have asked many people about the trajectory of life. Even my son understands the impact of the unpredictable. "I am reminded of an interview I did as a college student with a staff member, during an extremely brief stint at the school newspaper. As a result, he offered me a job as a web journalist...and eventually one as student web developer. A year after I graduated, he encouraged me to apply for my current position. If I hadn't met him during that "fluke" campus activity, I wouldn't be working where I am today!" Welcome to the feather-on-the-wind-life, son.

When asked, most people will admit their life landed in a place far removed from where they imagined it would. And if I listen very, very carefully, I often detect a tinge of guilt. "My life is good," they tell me, but their sub context is "but I was just so lucky. I benefited from so many flukes. I feel unworthy to take credit for the blessings I have been given."

So, in view of lives directed by the flight of swans, what do I tell my son about how to live the rest of his life?

I would be justified—and safe—if I were to pass along any number of well-worn pronouncements. "Those who fail to plan, plan to fail." "People who write down their goals are dramatically more successful than those who don't." "If we fail to study history we are doomed to repeat it." These, and thousands of others, are backed by data that appears to prove their validity. But I wonder.

These pieces of advice rely on skills that also seem somewhat well-worn. Describe the present state and create a vision of the future. It's then easy to identify the gap that emerges. Follow that with plans and endless "to-do" lists you can dutifully check off on the journey from today into the future. What we cannot take into account is that swans—be they black and horrific or white and joyous—have the irritating habit of showing up, making all the analysis and planning obsolete and sending us back to square one.

What then do we do—what alternate skills might we employ—to live in a world in which swans lurk around the very next corner? I can think of three. The first is to review where we have been, not as a detailed study of the events of the past, but in deep reflection. What has life taught me about who I am and what it means to be human? The second is the ability to "be" more and "do" less—we are, after all, as many have reminded me, human beings, not human doings. The last is the ability, desire and willingness to dream. As Dee Hock[11] has written, "At times such as these, it is no failure to fall short of realizing all that we might dream...the failure is to fall short of dreaming all that we might realize."

---

[11] Dee Hock is founder and CEO emeritus of Visa International and was named one of the "Great American Business Leaders of the 20th Century" by Harvard Business School. He is one of my greatest teachers, and one of the most erudite, wise and generous people I have ever had the pleasure to know.

One final story. I have struggled with these words—sat for hours trying to find the perfect metaphor. This morning I grabbed at random one of nearly 50 notes I received on a recent Snowball weekend. It was Jake's kind and generous note that ended up between my thumb and index finger. In that moment the winds of life had shown me the direction forward. I only needed to allow the words to appear over the horizon. And I arrived here without a beer, couch or television!

Surrender...It's Not for the Faint of Heart

"Try to get over the narrow idea that surrender is abject defeat. Surrender, in spirituality, is total acceptance."
From the Bhagavad Gita, as translated by Jack Hawley

When he finished playing, we embraced and I told him how he and his music have taught me a great deal about life.

Jeff has filled our house with music many times in the ten years since he and my daughter became friends. Typically, night has overtaken us as he sits gently on the piano bench. He asks if it's okay to turn down the lights; he prefers to play in near darkness. Within moments, he, the instrument and the music become one. I often wonder if he places his fingers on the keyboard, or if the keys reach upward to find him. In those moments, it seems music, piano, and musician relinquish individual identities and surrender to what is being called from them collectively. Jeff's hands and fingers move effortlessly, called into position by the music and the instrument that will declare it to the world. The experience often brings tears to my eyes.

I have a sense that if Jeff tried to rein in the music and piano, forcing them to do his bidding—failing to accept the latent invitation into the communal creation—the room would become infused with notes borne of conflict and control, rather than music that emanates from generosity, love and relationship.

We live in a world that would have me believe, with enough effort—more force and control—I can fill the future with music of my own making. I can rein in the world and make it do my bidding. Should I fail to align the world with my vision, it's solely due to a lack of effort and diligence. Jeff, the music, and the piano invite me to see the world in a new way: divine my path through surrender rather than diligence. In this world, I relinquish my individuality, accept the invitation to be found, and give of myself without reservation. When I find the courage required by surrender, the future arises from generosity, love and relationship...and is infinitely more beautiful than anything I could even imagine on my own.

The world of surrender, for me, is a brave new world...a truly foreign, oft-frightening, land. But in a book I read recently, the author suggested, in those moments when life offers comfort or fear, we should choose fear. Comfort confirms that which we already know. Fear offers the possibility of learning and wisdom. My real life exists in that brave new world, so here's to surrender, fear and courage.

Eroding the Riverbanks of Life

The flow of a river is constrained by its banks. Over time, however, the rushing water erodes the banks and redirects the course of the river. Riverbanks are necessary to give form, and yet the river retains the power to alter its future.

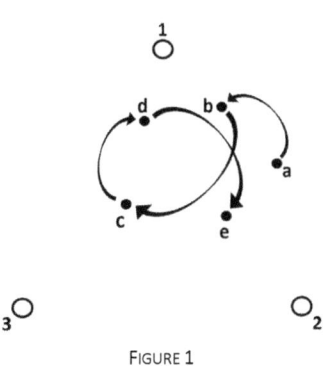

FIGURE 1

If you would be willing to play along, what appears as a game just may prompt surprising questions about the riverbanks that constrain our lives.

Mark three points on a piece of paper. Label them 1, 2 & 3. Pick *any* fourth point on the page—inside or outside the triangle, and find future points in the sequence using two simple rules: pick point 1, 2 or 3 at random and move 1/2 the distance from the most recent point toward the point you just chose. In Figure 1, I began at "a" and picked "1" at random. Point "b" is then 1/2 of the distance from "a" toward the number 1. Next, I picked "3" and moved 1/2 of the distance from "b" toward 3 to locate "c". Then I picked another "1," and moved 1/2 of the distance from "c" toward the number 1 to locate "d". Finally, I picked "2" and moved from "d" to locate "e," 1/2 of the way toward 2. Simple enough...go ahead and plot a hundred points or so. I'll wait...

If you did that, you would end up with a diagram similar to Figure 2. It appears a fairly random set of dots. What happens if you plot, say, 30,000? This time I won't wait. But before you look at the resulting diagram, any guesses what it might look like? Okay, take a look at the Sierpinski triangle (Figure 3) on page 120.

FIGURE 2

I find this result both stunning and terrifying.

I am stunned that such simple rules—rules that appear at first blush to yield chaos—countenance order and beauty over time. Order out of chaos. Stunning! Rules as simple as green means proceed, and red means wait, give order and meaning to millions of vehicles. "Do unto others…" gives order and meaning to our lives.

But there are ways in which I am terrified as well. As long as we remain allegiant to the rules, future dots are determined, and our path is immutable. We remain trapped in the pattern forever.

I wonder how I might remain trapped by rules in my life, even those so very subtle they remain imperceptible. Might there be ways in which my future is constrained, rigid and immutable? I hated to write essays in school and remained, for many years, certain of my inability to assemble meaningful words on paper. "I am a loner," "I am artistically destitute," "I am not a good listener," and "I don't like to read" defined much of my life. While I have not overcome feelings about lacking artistic ability, I have set aside many of the others.

I leave you with one final exercise. Allow yourself a few moments to reflect on the "rules" in your life. No doubt there are many that provide you with order and meaning. But if you are honest and look deeply enough, you just may uncover a few that keep you trapped in work, relationships, communities or images of self that limit your freedom, and constrain your future. It just might be time to jettison them, erode the riverbanks of your life and allow stunning new patterns to emerge.

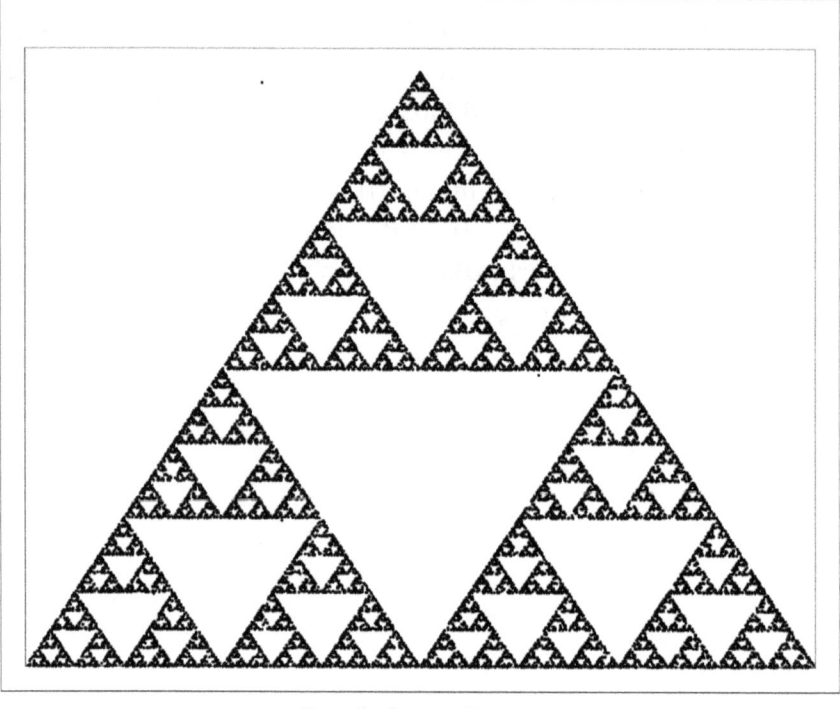

FIGURE 3 – SIERPINSKI TRIANGLE

The River of Life

The temporary nature of life exposes its most enduring value and meaning. A delicate, fragile piece of porcelain has more value because we realize the ease with which its beauty might be ripped from our lives at any moment. A vessel made virtually unbreakable would seldom etch the same splendor in our hearts.

So it is with the delicate nature of our relationships with those who know us and accept us for who we are. The value of those relationships in our lives is magnified by their impermanence; the magnificence of their unquestioning, unconditional love comes, in part, from its temporary, fragile nature.

If we could, would we return to an earlier time and cast-off the love, connection, and intimacy they offered in order to escape the pain and heartache that flows from having lost them? The answer is simple, but causes many to pause momentarily, especially in those moments when the sadness is fresh and the grief raw and unrelenting. In the end, we know that deep grief, and the tears that flow from it, are the price we pay for love.

It is said that a river cannot be halted in order to study its nature. When we fall under the spell of terrifying rapids, the melodious gurgle of a brook, or the majesty of water in free fall over a cliff, it is the impermanence, transformation and change that bind us to its beauty. If the current flowed forever without unexpected turns, protruding rocks, and the pull of gravity, we would never discern its power, elegance, and beauty.

Life itself is much like the ever-changing, impermanent flow of a river, but in life, we find ourselves unable to witness its power and splendor from afar. If we could, we might see the glory and majesty in a whole new way. Might the unexpected turns, the obstacles that rudely and harshly change our course, the free falls into an unknown abyss, contain a majesty we simply cannot comprehend as we are buffeted and battered by life?

With the perspective of time—more than ten years after his passing—I see the confluence and influence of my father's life with so much gratitude and love. I see him for the gracious, kind, caring person he strove to be, and forgive him for the times he was so very human...and fallible.

Regardless of our beliefs about what transpires after this time on Earth, each of us is granted a kind of immortality here, in this place. If "children are the messages we send to a time we will not see,"[12] when we live the messages of those who have come before us, we alter the flow of human history in their name. Even when life is punctuated with turns, boulders and freefalls, with perspective, we witness the river of life as a thing of true beauty, understand that impermanence imbues it with majesty, and know that those we have loved and lost helped make it so.

---

[12] See the essay "A Time I Will Not See" in the Second Inquiry.

On Being Fully Human

When I began this essay, I would have thought that being human and being inhuman were opposites and mutually exclusive. But now I wonder.

The spectrum of words that define "inhuman" range widely. At the brutal end are words like barbarism. At the softer end, even "lacking kindness, pity, or compassion" are invited to this party.

Steve Jobs was a creative genius, and he could ignite fire in those around him. And yet, his ability to frighten, intimidate and reduce others to tears is legendary.

Was this brutal side an integral part of his success? If someone had found a way to polish Jobs' rough edges—soften his abrupt, angry, impatient manner—might Apple have succumbed to one of its near-death incidents? After "Lisa" (a commercial failure in the 1980s), might Macintosh have remained only a variety of apple you eat? Might iPod, iPhone and iPad never have seen the light of iDay?

Did Jobs' willingness to reduce others to rubble better ensure Apple's innovations were more refined, dramatic and creative than they would have been if he treated product developers and researchers with kindness, pity and compassion? Did those invited to his office, knowing their careers could be made or broken by Jobs' quixotic reaction, work harder, refine further, create more before daring to walk under the transom?

The 1984 Los Angeles Olympics were organized under the attentive, uncompromising, often critical eye of Peter Ueberroth. Those Games were to become the first privately financed Games and resulted in a $250 million surplus that supported youth and sports activities across the United States. Compare that to the Montreal Games eight years earlier—or virtually any of the other modern games—which left that city burdened with debt for 30 years. For reimagining the financial foundation of the Games, and perhaps rescuing them from ruin, Ueberroth was awarded the Olympic Movement's highest honor: the Olympic Order in gold. He was named Time magazine's Man of the Year in 1984.

I once had the great joy of spending time with Dee Hock, one of the greatest businesspersons of the 20th century. Similar to Steve, Dee was a visionary and innovator. His ideas regarding the electronic transfer of money are arguably the precursor to all future forms of the transfer of value. If you read Dee's book *Birth of the Chaordic Age* (renamed and republished as *One from Many*) he too was very hard on those around him during his career. Like Jobs and Ueberroth, Dee had a vision that was so clear, so inviolate, that compromise was simply not possible. When I asked him why, he looked at me and said, "I had a sense that if I didn't take a stand, something in me would die."

I hold each of these leaders in the highest esteem. Each opened doors to innovation that might have remained closed for many years without them. And yet, each let some edges of inhumanity slip into their lives. Or perhaps, our definitions of inhuman simply do not allow us to be fully human.

A Message 500 Years in the Making

They laid the first stone April 14, 1434—three hundred and forty two years before America's Declaration of Independence. It took 50 years just to complete the façade. Inauguration of the nave and aisles occurred in the late 1500s. On December 25, 1891, 457 years after they began, Bishop Jules François Lecoq inaugurated the completed St. Peter and St. Paul's cathedral in Nantes, France.

On a recent visit with our daughter after her semester abroad, I stood in the nave of this edifice, gazing upward 114 feet to the roof. The interior is 116 feet wide and 313 feet long. The outside towers rise 192 feet. These somewhat cold statistics cannot begin to instill the awe that overwhelms you as you stand in this glorious holy space.

As I stood in this vessel—a message sent from the Middle Ages, and delivered to me in this moment—I realize the stones in the columns beside me were carefully, perhaps lovingly, put in place by a mason more than 500 years ago. My mind is flooded with questions I fear we have lost the ability to answer. When we find it difficult to create plans that survive four decades, how was it possible 600 years ago to design a structure that would not be completed for more than four centuries—and last a thousand years? In an environment in which every generation is encouraged to leave their unique fingerprint on the future, how did more than 20 generations refrain from changing the cathedral's original design? When the technologies we use to transmit information to the future change every 2 or 3 years, can we even conceive of passing plans entrusted to fragile parchment across more than 400?

However, the questions that most intrigue me relate to the mason who laid the stones in front of me—perhaps a hundred years after construction began. Even if he began as an apprentice and spent the entirety of his life dedicated to the completion of this monument to his creator, it would have risen only a few meters as he lay on his deathbed. He woke every morning, and invested all of himself for his entire life, inspired only by a vision of this gift to generations so distant their lives were simply unimaginable. Would any of us be willing to toil for our entire lives on a project begun by our great, great, great, great, great grandparents, which would not be completed before the birth of our great, great, great, great, great grandchildren?

In an ironic coincidence, I began reading *Christianity: The First Three Thousand Years* by Diarmaid MacCulloch before we began our two-week pilgrimage. As MacCulloch relates the history and derivation of the Christian faith, he touches on the origin, meaning and symbolism of the world's great cathedrals. As I read MacCulloch's words and chapters, and stroll the masons' nave and aisles, I am struck by the juxtaposition of the creation of a cathedral and the formation of humankind's great wisdom traditions. Each is a gift from the past, built from seemingly infinite, small, often courageous contributions by mostly anonymous individuals.

I am left to imagine generations 600 years hence. What will they come to know of us? What messages will we have left behind that speak of our visions and passions? Are we building any edifice—with the bricks we lay or the wisdom we formulate—that will invite them into a feeling of awe?

Then the final questions emerge: What have I done, what will I do today, and to what will I dedicate my remaining days to help craft a message of wisdom, to be left for my great, great, great, great, great grandchildren? The masons of the 15th century had answers we may have forgotten.

Kicking and Screaming

When my parents turned 75, I asked to sit with them and capture a few memories. I hoped to wander the peaks and valleys of their journey; peering into their lives and helping them recall wisdom they surely received over seven and a half decades.

They eventually acquiesced, but not before disavowing any particular insight into what it means to be human. In the midst of the negotiation, a friend said "Ask them if they simply want to be older, or would they rather be elders."

Older or elder. Change a single letter, and the words suddenly compete for the definitive description of what it means to enter the most senior years of a human's time on Earth.

Many older people have either learned to deny their wisdom or are so certain of it they populate their discourse with an overabundance of sentences ending with periods. Their ideas are correct, indisputable and change more slowly than Earth's tectonic plates collide. The fields where their discussions take root are arid and choked with weeds; not an environment where a delicate new idea might find nourishment. And when life comes to an end, they often leave kicking and screaming.

On the other hand, I know many seniors who don't need to deny or declare their wisdom. Through the subtlety and openness afforded by question marks, their intellectual gardens nurture new species of mental flora or fauna. They are the elders who have planted seeds of wisdom in my life.

In a recent discussion with friends, we explored the myriad roots and meanings of the word "wisdom". One image emerged in the midst of the conversation: a wise person is perpetually in an honest, deeply inquisitive relationship with the world as it arises in front of them. Such a person approaches every moment with the eyes of a child...in wonderment and amazement. They have the stunning ability to bring their years of experience to each moment, making it more extraordinary, but don't allow the learnings from their yesterdays to blind them to some subtle newness that may avail itself tomorrow. They are aware that every moment offers the possibility of an idea, thought or experience without precedent in their life, or perhaps even in the life of all humanity.

Why the ruminations about elderhood versus olderhood? I awoke early this morning to wander this path because today is the 60th anniversary of the day I arrived on this planet. And while I don't remember, I'm sure I arrived as most do, literally kicking and screaming.

I am more aware than ever that I am dipping my toes into the senior years of my life. And so, I too must begin to ask if I desire the wisdom and grace of elderhood, or am I destined to become stuck in the intellectual drought that results from the overuse of declarations...and scarcity of question marks. Should I live to see the completion of 70 or 80 years, will I have developed an honest, deeply inquisitive relationship with the world as it arises in front of me? Will I learn to experience the world with a gentle sense of wonderment, amazement and perhaps a bit of wisdom?

Or will I leave as I arrived...kicking and screaming?

Regret at the End of Life

Steven Covey, author of *The Seven Habits of Highly Effective People*, said it whimsically: few people on their deathbed wish they had spent more time at the office. But recent encounters leave me reflecting, considerably less whimsically, on what I might wish for the moments just before I am called from this life.

For many years, I have facilitated a Socrates Café. We spend our time together exchanging thoughts and exploring the nuance of language related to whatever happens to nip at us as we gather.

In the middle of one Café, a nurse began to speak softly about having been with hundreds the moment they passed from this life to the next. "The expression I see most often as a life ends is regret. It is as if they are asking 'Is this all my life amounts to?' My goal is to not die with a look of regret on my face." The rest of us could do little more than quietly take in the reality of her experience. Is it true at the moment of passing most people regret, rather than appreciate, their lives? Is it natural to focus on the empty moments rather than those that fulfill us and those around us? I left the Café disturbed.

Two weeks later, we continued to explore the question of regret at the end of life. Perhaps, I suggested, it is not wrong to leave this life with regret. Others recalled how humans have a natural desire to achieve and create...to leave this place better as a result of our journey. Does the endless longing to create insure there will be things undone no matter when our life ends, and that regret over the undone will animate our neurons as they fire for the last time?

In the Sioux tradition there is a battle cry, "I am ready for whatever comes." It is often translated poorly and credited to Crazy Horse as "Today is a good day to die." The group reflected on what it might mean for today to be a good day to die. The nurse who started us down this extraordinary path suggested it might be powerful for each of us to seek the answer privately. "If you can answer 'yes,' it might be valuable to reflect on the aspects of life that give you emotional permission to say that if life ended today, it would feel complete, satisfying and fulfilled."

In between the two Cafés, I was with a group challenged by the following quirky question: "If you could have a superpower, what would it be?" The suggestions were fun and imaginative. Teleportation, the ability to fly or read others' minds were among the most popular. But it was those that dealt with time that gave me pause: "I'd like to be able to do two things at once…slow down time…turn back time…get by on one or two hours of sleep." I began to wonder what lay at the heart of such desires. Is a wish for more time an indicator I am dissatisfied with what I have done with the time already spent? Does such a wish silently scream that what I have done—or even worse, who I am—is not enough? Is my endless list of to-dos really that important? And how many of the items on that list are there to assuage my fragile ego rather than meet the world's great needs? Is it possible to lay head against pillow each night with a deep sense that what was done that day was enough?

So what do I wish as this life reaches its conclusion? The same things I wish each night as I lay head against pillow: that I am wise enough to have salved wounds I might have opened, to have told those around me how much they have meant on my journey and to know that in some small ways the balance of good and bad in my life tips more toward the good. If I have met the world's great need in some small way, perhaps, in those final moments, I will feel my life will have been enough.

Fifth Inquiry:
Our Individual & Collective Journeys

> *"We're so engaged in doing things to achieve purposes of outer value that we forget the inner value. The rapture that is associated with being alive, is what it is all about."*
> Joseph Campbell

The rapture of being alive. How often do I allow myself to live into the joy, ecstasy or bliss available every moment? Will I breathe my last breath with a profound understanding of the rapture of life, or will my life—overly filled with plans, goals, lists of things to do—be defined by living the incumbent terror of failing in those endeavors.

Lives are bounded, defined and animated by their brevity. It matters not whether one's lifespan is 20, 75 or 375 years, so long as earthly life is finite, we exist with a kind of desperation that arises from that finitude. Even if a belief in eternal life, or in countless earthly lives through reincarnation, offers a bit of comfort, I, like most humans, cling desperately to *this* time on Earth.

Not only do we cling to this infinitesimally short journey, we are in desperate search for its meaning. It was because of this desperation that I once sponsored a series of dialogues entitled "Death as a Spiritual Teacher." It was a short time for humans to gather in a circle and open ourselves to the grief we feel about the preciousness of life as it slips through our fingers. Why are we here? Why am I here as an individual? Why are we here as a species? Why is there something at all rather than nothing?

And yet, despite an abiding desire to discover meaning, we waste far too much of our lives in search of the meaningless. Viktor Frankl said, "Ever more people today have the means to live, but no meaning to live for." Is all the stuff of my life, the mountains of things that comprise my "means to live," necessary? Is the extraordinary amount of time I spend accumulating things justifiable, if, on my deathbed, I have found little or no meaning to my existence?

I recall an interview with a dear friend, Kathie Dannemiller. Kathie was a pioneer in understanding the complexity of organizations, and helped us see how they can come alive when we understand what truly animates communal labor. She spent her life helping organizations find collective meaning, and helping every individual who plays a role find the personal meaning of their labor and unique gifts. Kathie changed the lives of countless thousands. Her passion, love and generosity changed lives like mine in profound ways. And yet, she told me with deeply sad eyes, "I don't want my life to have been a throwaway line."

How might we better help each other uncover the meaning of our lives, individually and collectively? From the moment of conception, how might we honor our children's path to find their unique gifts—the majesty they were sent here to live? How might we cultivate fertile ground that will enable them to blossom?

At the same time, as we discover the power of living into the gifts we were sent here to share, can we re-member we are part of an enormous, complex community—a global life force that we cannot, nor should we, wish to control? Can we learn to stand in the humility required of us in the face of the beauty and complexity that is Gaia[13]?

Was there a time in which humans moved more gracefully, albeit treacherously, in time with the rhythm of

---

[13] The Gaia hypothesis was first proposed by James Lovelock. It postulates that the Earth functions as a self-regulating, living system.

the Universe? I wonder if humans of an earlier age, because more of their lives were etched by deep pain, horrific suffering and excruciating heartache, understood something of the human journey that I can no longer fathom. Don't misunderstand, I am caught in the paradox I just described. I wouldn't survive a single day of that life. The infinitely easier lives we lead, have been a wonderful gift, but I am aware that the price we pay, in terms of lost wisdom, is also steep.

When I walk in the woods, I am reminded how much of nature still exists in the unrelenting severity humans have endeavored to escape. Yet, in the harsh reality of nature, communication, communion and generosity of spirit are everywhere to witness. I often stand with my hand gently touching a tree, trying to understand the majesty and generosity of such a living organism. A tree blossoms, lives and dies with a single purpose: to give of what it has and to take only that which it needs to sustain life. If I peer carefully, insects of all kinds use the tree—its bark, branches and leaves—for home and for food. Underground, I am told the root system is every bit as large as what I can see above ground, and those roots participate in a community of living beings. Each plays its part...each giving what it can and taking what it needs, and little more.

Might that be true for us as well? How is it humans have so lost their place in that community? How have we become so demanding and selfish? Must we, in the end, return to an understanding our distant relatives might have shared, that we are here to give our gifts and take only that which sustains us? From where I peer at this point, such an understanding seems incomprehensible.

The essays in this Fifth Inquiry take a whirlwind tour of the human journey from the individual to the collective.

In "Orchids and Roses" I am humbled by the uniqueness of my children and my need to honor who they are in the face of who I might wish them to become. What is my role as parent and care-giver? I ask "Are they in my life to teach me something about the unimaginable mystery, miracle and beauty of this Universe?"

Then, in "The Miracle of Life," I recall what we have gained, and what we may have lost as the health and well-being of our children has become so much more certain. I mourn for parents of an earlier age who buried so many of their youth...and I wonder if they held young life in their hands and hearts with greater respect, care and affection because it was, for them, so much more fragile. As we have made life less fragile, have we given up some measure of profound respect for its magnificence?

It is a great conundrum that, as life expectancy grows, we remain deeply dissatisfied with the length of time we are allowed on this planet. I am certain a life of 300 years, should it become the norm, would still seem far too short, and would further allow us to waste the moments that truly change the course of history. I explore the implications of lifespan in "A Single Day of Eternity." Regardless of the moments I have left, do I endeavor to honor each one and use it with wisdom and generosity?

Humans have, through the ages, sought meaning and fulfillment. The paradox is that as we have accumulated wealth, self-worth can become increasingly elusive. "Being Exhausted Before Life Ends" is an exploration of what it might mean to find and give of our gifts, rather than focusing on building greater wealth. I wonder if I will have discovered all that I have to give, and then to have given every bit, as I lay on my deathbed.

In "Humanity on the Cusp" I compare an individual's "hero's journey," with the journey on which the species is embarking. We gain individual wisdom by living through the suffering of the journey of life. Joseph Campbell reminded us of the value of the hero's journey—the decent into the darkness, only to return with many scars and much greater wisdom. I suspect the species is about to gain great wisdom in the face of our collective hero's journey.

Many years ago, my brother-in-law took us onto the lava flows of Hawai'i. He cautioned us to be aware of the heat we might feel as we traversed rocks that might have been molten a few hours earlier, and be prepared to "move to a different rock." So too for humanity. Might the belief systems and values on which we build our future actually burn our soles…and souls? "Moving to a Different Rock" outlines that journey. I wonder if the species *Homo Sapiens* will have the courage and fortitude, in the end, to find the voice of welcoming, generosity, grace and wisdom of which we are capable.

Orchids and Roses

One weekend, my wife and I joined our children in the Quad Cities of Illinois and Iowa, our son's adopted home, for a new tradition of enjoying their many pre-holiday events. If you haven't been there, I recommend it.

All weekend, the two of us sat in amazement in the presence of our children. I know they are no more amazing than millions of other emerging young adults, but since they are my children I demand the right to be in awe of who they are becoming, and speak of them as if they truly are God's gift...because to me they are. *What can bring me to my knees, is wondering why I have been given the gift of them in my life.*

After expressing my disbelief on a social media page, a dear friend commented, in part, "Seems to me 'everything' the two of you did as parents explains their beauty." I appreciate the generosity, but can my efforts—occasionally kind, gentle and loving, but so often tinged by personal struggles and imperfections—explain the beauty in front of me this past weekend? As hard as I tried, as much as I wished to be a perfect parent, I grieve over the endless times I failed. I am saddened by the hundreds of times they longed for a listening and compassionate ear, and I found it necessary instead to attempt to fix or teach. I lament how often the stress of my life intruded on theirs in the form of unjustified anger and frustration. I mourn the lost opportunities when a different kind of attention would have nourished them in more abundant ways. And yet, in spite of my failings, they emerge as caring, compassionate, fervent young adults.

My wife has a growing passion, and a passion for growing, orchids. Last week, after more than a year, she coaxed one of her plants into rewarding us with three absolutely gorgeous blooms. They are stunning. And while I do not want to demean the loving care she gave them, their beauty is far greater than the effort to raise it. A bit of care, some water and a nourishing environment yield a thing of stunning beauty. The orchid rushes forth, becoming what it was always intended to be so long as it has a healthy environment and nothing gets in the way of its journey from seed to blossom. The grandeur of the blossom is contained in the tiny seed from which it grows. No matter how hard she might have tried, no matter the extent of her care or the nourishment she provided, could she have coaxed the orchid plant into producing roses? Anything she might have done to try would surely have damaged this thing of beauty.

When people tell us we did a wonderful job raising our children, I usually reflect that if we did anything well, perhaps we stayed out of their way just enough. We tried to provide a loving, nourishing environment, but we always knew they had to blossom into the amazing humans they were intended to be; an orchid if it was their birthright or a rose if that's what was implanted in their soul.

So why have I been given the gift of these two amazing people in my life? Maybe, just maybe, they weren't put here for me to be the teacher, but the learner. Are they in my life to teach me something about the unimaginable mystery, miracle and beauty of this Universe? This weekend was a magnificent lesson and I am grateful beyond words.

The Miracle of Life

As we approach the 4th of July, my thoughts turn to the founding of this nation, and a person I particularly admire: Thomas Jefferson. I admire his wisdom and depth of knowledge across many disciplines. In this moment, however, what gives me pause is not his insight into the failure of the Divine Right of Kings and emergence of democracy. I am reflecting on what I can only imagine was his, and his wife Martha's deep understanding of the value of human life.

Martha Jefferson had seven children. John Skelton, conceived with her first husband, died at the age of three the summer before she married Thomas Jefferson. Of the six children she bore in her ten-year marriage to Thomas, only two daughters, Martha and Mary lived into adulthood. Two daughters and a son died as infants. The sixth died of whooping cough at the tender age of two.

Burying children must be one of the most difficult things any parent can do in life. Today, we consider it to be contrary to that natural order, but in times past, it was certainly not unusual.

For most of human history, life expectancy has been short...perhaps 25 years for our hunter-gatherer ancestors. During the early 1600s in England, life expectancy was only about 35 years, largely because two-thirds of all children died before the age of four. Life expectancy was under 25 years in the Colony of Virginia, and in seventeenth-century New England, about 40% died before reaching adulthood.

I wonder, as a result, if our ancestral parents had a very different sense of the miracle of life. Did living with such a profound understanding of life's fragility permit them to look upon their adult children with deeper appreciation and love?

My wife and I have two children. In the years since our son was born, I spent few moments worrying about his or his sister's successful journey into adulthood. Medical science gifted us with a sense of safety, and belief in the vigor, rather than fragility, of human life. I always believed, regardless the malady, a trip to the doctor or the emergency room would present an appropriate remedy.

Would my relationship with them be different if we had had six children and buried four of them before two of them reached adulthood? How could it not be? How could I not see them as even more miraculous than I do now? How could I not worry every day I might yet have to lay one or both of them to rest before my life ends?

Not long ago, I was introduced to a man whose 18-month old son succumbed to sudden infant death. My heart breaks for him. But it cannot possibly break in the same wrenching way it would if I had shared the horrific experience of having to say goodbye to a child.

I am thankful there are support groups for parents who have lost children. But in this age, a grieving parent must search for others who share their unimaginable pain and heartbreak. Martha and Thomas did not have to search for support groups that would gather from hither and yon. In virtually every direction, there were others who shared intimately in their loss. Caring hands and hearts were everywhere. No matter where they traveled, there were others who understood, as did they, just how astonishing and miraculous human life truly is.

Do I wish a return to a time of ever present grief from the loss of children? No, I certainly do not. But I am aware of the paradox that, in our safety and comfort, we have surrendered some amount of wisdom and appreciation—perhaps significant amount—for the miracle of life itself.

A Single Day of Eternity

The moment of turning the calendar from one year to the next gives me pause. I wonder if I will have left a legacy. Will I have helped move humanity forward, or might my life have been, as a dear friend once fretted, a throwaway line? I ponder the best way to spend the 365 days I gently step into on January 1.

In those moments, an image painted by Hendrik Willem van Loon in his wonderful book, *The Story of Mankind*, comes to mind:

"High up in the North in the land called Svithjod, there stands a rock. It is a hundred miles high and a hundred miles wide. Once every thousand years a little bird comes to this rock to sharpen its beak. When the rock has thus been worn away, a single day of eternity will have gone by.

We live under the shadow of a gigantic question mark.

Who are we? Where do we come from? Whither are we bound?

Slowly, but with persistent courage, we have been pushing this question mark further and further towards that distant line, beyond the horizon, where we hope to find our answer.

We have not gone very far."

I find this image of a single day of eternity compelling. In the face of an eternity this unimaginable, I feel small and insignificant.

I recall standing in the presence of the Giant Sequoias in California and marveling that many have lived thousands of years. Many were alive through the entirety of the Current Era. They lived through the Roman Empire, the Renaissance, the Middle Ages and the rise and fall of the Divine Right of Kings. To them, the ink on our Declaration of Independence has yet to dry. American representative governance, the World Wars, the Holocaust, the Vietnam War happened moments ago. And yet, even to them, van Loon's "single day of eternity" is unimaginable.

Then, imagine living the life of a mayfly—often a single day. As you begin to mature by mid-morning, you wonder about the species' evolution. You see so many ways in which it falls short of the enlightened state of which you dream. By midday you are working tirelessly for the betterment of your fellow mayflies. Within hours, as you age, you become distraught because, in spite of your lifetime of dedication and effort, little has changed. The species is no less selfish…its lifespan hasn't increased…there is no less violence between you and those with whom you compete for resources. You wonder if there is any hope for the future. I imagine *that* species is awed that a human such as myself has witnessed tens of thousands of their generations.

We might witness the mayfly and smile. How silly to imagine, that in such a short lifetime, an insect could hope to actually witness evolution! Then I wonder if the Sequoia looks at us with the same mix of wonder, whimsy and pity.

And yet, as humans, we live with the hubris to imagine that in our lifetime, or certainly within a few generations, we will experience the advancement of our species into something significantly new and wonderful. Not only do we expect to have witnessed advances in evolution, we believe we will have personally contributed to forward movement so significant we can actually witness growth. Then, as we age, we become distraught because, in spite of a lifetime of dedication and effort, little has changed. The species is no less selfish...its lifespan hasn't increased...there is no less violence between us and those with whom we compete for resources. We wonder if there is any hope for the future.

If it is naive to expect my life will make a noticeable difference in the course of human history, what then? How should I decide what to do, how shall I spend the moments I am given in the year ahead?

One answer to that question, and there are many, rests in the flapping wings of butterflies. The Butterfly Effect, as mentioned before, tells us that a minute air disturbance in one part of the world can, through a complex and unpredictable chain of events, foster a tornado halfway around the globe. And the butterfly that set the future in motion has no idea of its impact thousands of miles away and months or years later.

The future unfolds based on "initial conditions." An infinitesimally small change in this moment, can, as a "single day of eternity" transpires, allow an entirely new, dramatically different future to blossom.

So what I think about, as I step into the 365 days that begin on the first of January, is what initial conditions am I creating in this moment? Is the wisp of air I am disturbing filled with joy, kindness and generosity, or anger and hate? Am I aware of the pain and heartache in the face of the stranger next to me, or am I focused on me and my needs? What can I do in this moment to give the future the very best foundation on which to begin its next "day of eternity"? My stay on this Earth is far too short to witness the impact of the initial conditions I set, so all I can do is have faith that the future will best be served if I serve this moment in the most loving and attentive way I can.

So for me, life is a constant struggle to meet, and negotiate with, each and every moment. As I approach the next moment, I hope to serve it the best I can as I inhabit it, and it inhabits me. And then, perhaps, I must simply trust that the "single day of eternity," of which we both become a part, will take care of itself.

Being Exhausted Before Life Ends

"Most writing is the scratching of an insatiable itch for immortality. Alas, the more written, the greater the itch."
Dee Hock

Since reading Dee's most recent work, *Autobiography of a Restless Mind*, I have been pondering the human desire for immortality, and wondering if, perhaps, we understand immortality inaccurately.

2.2 million books were published last year. As of this writing, 152 million blogs pepper the Internet. Two are added every second...63 million per year. WordPress, one of many blogging sites, documents 2 million posts every day. And these figures ignore journals, periodicals, newspapers and editorials.

If Dee is correct, the itch for immortality is indeed insatiable and growing at an unprecedented rate.

It would be convenient to claim I am unmotivated by Dee's itch, but it would be disingenuous. Who amongst us, when mortality tugs at our coattails, can make an honest claim to nary a qualm? Has it always been so?

The period from 800 B.C.E to 200 B.C.E., often referred to as the Axial Age, was a time of great change. Prior to the Axial Age it was impossible to imagine individuals separate from their tribe. With no stored wealth, and each day's survival in question, the effort of every member was essential. If the tribe was to survive, each person's gifts and capacities had to be discovered, honored and engaged. *Every person mattered.*

With the advent of the Axial Age, cities emerged and wealth accumulated. Families and individuals could, for the first time, survive independent of the tribe. Wealth lubricated, if you will, families from many of the day-to-day terrors that made the lives of their ancestors so precarious. But with life becoming safer and a tad easier, individuals and their unique gifts became less important for survival. Perhaps for the first time in our history, individuals might have begun to wonder if they were necessary.

The Axial Age was also an astounding time in the development of human wisdom. Socrates, Plato and Aristotle laid the groundwork for much of the West's rational, scientific views. The Buddha proposed his ideas for reincarnation, and an end to human suffering through non-attachment. Jainism gave us the principles of non-violence, karma and asceticism. The Upanishads, the Tao, the Iliad, the Odyssey and the Bhagavad Gita were written during this period. Confucius, Archimedes, Elijah and Isaiah are also considered to be of this age.

Is it coincidence that, facing the possibility this life might be meaningless, desires for immortality emerged, and definitions and descriptions flourished? For Buddhists, immortality was realized by reincarnation through many lives, eventually reaching an unending state of Nirvana. The monotheistic religions (Judaism, Islam and Christianity) found comfort in a single life with a heavenly destination in which we could spend eternity in bliss reunited with our maker. The Greeks found a form of immortality through *thumos*, recognition and fame that would secure a person's place on the lips and in the hearts of future generations.

If there is any veracity to the claim that riches and an easy life can make self-worth elusive, our craving for immortality is exacerbated by our unimaginable collective wealth, and our belief that medicine, science and technology will make life safer, easier and perhaps even everlasting. It's paradoxical I admit, but, as life becomes safer and easier, could it mean that each of us matters even less? And if so, might the quest for life's meaning become excruciatingly difficult, elusive and painful?

I know this: I talk to many people for whom life has become unbearable for one simple reason—their life has no meaning. They have given up the search for the gifts that make them unique and magnificent. The tribe no longer needs them.

So I wonder. Is it possible the only immortality—unending existence—that truly matters, is in discovering our gifts and being fully exhausted of them by life's end…knowing they have been given in service to the human tribe. Perhaps immortality and humility emerge from gently etching our irreplaceable footprint on the human journey as the tribe searches for a sustainable path into the future.

Humanity on the Cusp

Humanity is, I believe, on the cusp of a new era. Depending on the choices we make, the future will be informed by wisdom beyond our dreams, or imbued with ignorance and wanting.

Am I alone in feeling that many of our species' collective actions seem self-centered and selfish? It's as if we are still in our adolescence searching for identity. We grab Earth's resources because exerting power over Mother Earth—or as I prefer, Pachamama—affirms an identity we doubt.

Mythologist Joseph Campbell spoke of the hero's journey, an individual's passage through the depths and darkness, emerging on the other side with wisdom, the profundity of which can only come from the struggle. What most separates youth from elderhood is a deep understanding and acceptance of self, much of which comes from the many struggles through which we visit the depths and return, burnished, refined and wiser...less ego-imbued, self-centered and selfish.

The people we embrace as wisdom keepers throughout history were, at some point, torn asunder by journeys of nearly unfathomable pain and heartbreak, only to return with an extraordinary understanding of what it means to be human. Mahatma Gandhi's and Nelson Mandela's ego-crushing years in prison come to mind.

As a species, we have faced many journeys through the darkness: world wars, genocides, famines and natural disasters. We have gained wisdom from each, but we seem to forget so rapidly, returning to wasteful, selfish ways—

ignorant of the delicate, life-giving balance of the planet. Today, we deplete precious resources at increasingly alarming rates.

Perhaps the hero's journey that will provide lasting wisdom—move us closer to elderhood of the species—is yet to come.

My brother-in-law, Professor Emeritus of Geology at the University of Hawai'i, has spoken of a world depleted of oil...a world he feels is approaching swiftly, much sooner than we can find alternatives. Having read and listened, it is an often frightening picture that can include famine, institutional collapse and chaos. Edward O. Wilson, Professor Emeritus from Harvard, once referred to the 21st century as the bottleneck humanity must negotiate if we are to survive.

I wonder if what lies ahead is a collective hero's journey unlike those through which we have already traversed. A journey that will refine and burnish the species in ways we cannot yet imagine. If such a journey is in our future, I also wonder if we will find the courage to endure the depths required for our resurrection as wiser, more mature inhabitants of the Earth...to move as a species from adolescence into elderhood.

If we do find the courage to make generosity and compassion our dominant voice, those moments are perhaps the greatest opportunities we have ever had for acquiring wisdom. If we do not, I fear we will never advance beyond our current selfish ignorance.

If the hero's journey I am suggesting transpires, we are approaching a time during which we can allow Pachamama to extract from us, individually and collectively, the infinite wisdom of which we are capable. The next century offers us an advanced degree in existentialism. Why do we exist?

Do we truly belong here in this Universe? And if we do, what is our role and how should we be in relation to life itself?

That future holds for all creatures, riches of joy, wisdom, generosity, understanding and love beyond anything we have ever imagined, or ever could imagine. Will we get there without pain, heartache, suffering and sadness? That would contradict the very definition of wisdom. Will the riches we will discover be commensurate with the heartache and suffering we may face? Not only is it possible, I believe the wisdom available to us far exceeds the price we will be asked to pay.

I fervently believe it is human nature to be generous rather than selfish. When we stop long enough to re-connect with parts of the biosphere from which we have become aliens, I hope we will re-member we are part of a much larger whole.

I must have hope. Because if I lose hope, what have I left?

Moving to a Different Rock

Years ago, my brother-in-law, a retired geophysicist, invited us to join him on a trek across the lava on the island of Hawai'i so we could see red-hot flows scorching their way to the ocean—nature's way of making the Big Island even bigger.

The hike was several miles without the aid of a trail. Having spent many hours on the flows, my brother-in-law had many words of advice—but it was his final admonition, as we came within a few feet of the blazing river of lava, that lodged itself in a deep crevice in my brain. Since even the "cooled" lava had been molten not long before our visit, he warned, "If your feet get warm, move to a different rock." There's wise but useless counsel, I thought. Who would stand motionless in life as the soles of their shoes begin to burn?

I wonder if the same is true for humans as a species. To believe we can continue on our current path is folly. Our collective feet are getting warm—as is the global environment. How long can we keep from being scorched by an economic system based on digging up resources we turn into temporary trinkets to use briefly, discard and bury? How we will continue to feed 7 billion people, even as we become 12 billion, as farmland is increasingly turned into strip malls and housing developments? But then, to save corporate mega-farms is to preserve a different kind of ecological disaster. How long will Mother Nature—Pachamama—put up with a species that shows so little regard for the delicate balance required to support all life?

At what point might she call a halt to our self-centeredness?

Our current thinking, and what flows from our thoughts, is in profound misalignment with the natural cycles of life. To continue thinking in Newtonian ways about how to "fix" Pachamama will further heat the rocks on which we stand. Our future depends on our willingness to be in, and of, this world—partner with Pachamama—in ways that are far more than adaptations of our current ways of thinking and doing. Our Newtonian infused minds want to plan, organize and manipulate—forge a future we believe is knowable and predictable. What if, we must instead, allow new visions of the world, and humankind's role in it, to emerge slowly, and in unpredictable ways?

An image returns from my trip to Hawai'i. As I stood amid the endless black landscape, I beheld a tiny green shoot that found its way through the lava. It was there not because it planned, manipulated and organized, but simply by being there to rebuild the tropical paradise.

Humanity has always known how to be in the world; perhaps we have simply forgotten. The biologists Humberto Maturana and Francisco Verela, in studying living systems, learned that health can be restored to an ailing system only by reconnecting it with more of itself. What would it mean for us to reconnect with other parts of the living system known as Gaia? Can we learn to listen more deeply for what is trying to be born? Can we hear what life is asking of us rather than telling life what we expect from it? Is it time we remembered ways of listening that transcend the rational mind; ways that penetrate our hearts as well as our minds? What if returning home means we need to stop, listen and allow the Universe to find us. Do we have that much courage?

The next moments in human history offer boundless opportunities for learning and wisdom. We are standing upon a welcome mat, inviting us to co-create with Pachamama the next epoch of her future—not a future separate from humanity, and not a future for humanity separate from her. We are poised to rediscover our place as an important, but far-from-dominant species, and help create a future for a global life force, fully integrated, and intimately intertwined.

On a walk up the steep volcanic slopes of O'ahu, I struggled to navigate a narrow, craggy, roadside path to avoid trampling a beautiful, carefully cultivated garden on the other side of the road. An elder, tending to the lush beauty, called to me; "Please, walk here; it is safer." If, collectively, we can find that voice of welcoming, generosity, grace and wisdom—and if that should become the dominant song of our species—perhaps, in the end, there is hope.

*The Continuing Inquiry:
Could We See It Another Way?*

The 14-year-old who called the suicide hotline was in desperate need of healing and self-absolution. I realize now, the seed of the conversation we shared was planted nearly 40 years ago.

After finishing my master's degree, I was invited to teach mathematics at a private, preparatory school just outside of Princeton, NJ. Teaching encompassed four years of my life, but, for my students, I will have been their math teacher for the entirety of theirs. When you fail in many endeavors, there is often a remedy. When you fail as a teacher, your students live with your ineptitude until the day they pass from this Earth.

I often felt inept…unpolished…incapable of reaching the students who struggled mightily with algebra, geometry and trigonometry. Often, they needed a guide with great patience, and I came up short. Those failures weigh heavily even 40 years later.

A note recently left on my website, reminded me of moments in which, perhaps, I was less inept. I was touched by the memories it evoked. The missive was from a former student who arrived from Iran in his junior year. I could present him as proof of my success as a teacher, but this young man would have excelled with nearly any teacher. He worked diligently, but he had an innate aptitude for mathematics. He and a few of his peers easily opened their minds to the concepts behind the numbers and the theory.

Despite their innate ability, I remember one or two moments when these students came with a question, standing on the precipice of understanding, but not quite over the edge. In those moments, we would engage with the mathematics; when understanding eluded us we would ask each other if we could possibly see the problem another way. As we challenged each other to look anew, there would come a moment when their eyes—or mine—would light up as we completed a critical neural pathway and a new piece of the puzzling language of mathematics fell into place. Those moments too, I remember 40 years later.

I had no idea how central to my very being the idea of seeing another way would become. A young boy who called the suicide hotline was wracked by disease. The ensuing bullying from both peers and self, demarcated a life of failure, pain and self-loathing. And yet, every story he recounted spoke of his caring, generosity and fierce defense of loved ones. Late in our time together, I asked him to describe something, anything, wonderful within. "I can't," he told me in a soft voice. "I hate everything about myself." So I began to recount his stories of caring, generosity and love, and asked if he could witness, not shortcomings, but his huge heart. "It's your superpower," I suggested. I also told him I loved him, and who he is in the world. Near tears he told me those were words he seldom hears. "Would you be willing to see your life through your enormous heart?" I asked just before the call ended. "Thank you, I will try," were his final words before we ended our time together.

Should We See It Another Way?

The question begs another: What is the "It" to which I refer?

The "It" to which I refer is fully inclusive. I can think of little in all human experience, knowledge, perception, or wisdom that we should allow to slip from our inquisitive purview. I have come to know that virtually everything I have thought, felt and believed in my lifetime has been altered by the battering ram of deep inquiry. Perhaps "battering ram" sounds overly violent, and, while wisdom sometimes enters my world quiescently, the most meaningful insights disrupt my thinking and beliefs in radical and profoundly disturbing ways.

When I enter each day with a sense of wonder—with a mind willing to question old beliefs and see anew—I am gifted with learning and insights from people with extraordinary wisdom—those who call the suicide hotline and allow me a brief portal into their oft-difficult world...teens in Operation Snowball who instruct me in the art of living in the face of deep pain and despair...my friends at the Socrates Café who challenge each other to peer ever more deeply into what we do not yet know. I have come to understand that the only certainty in life is there is nothing certain. If there is naught yet to be discovered, if I am destined to see in twenty years, *exactly* as I see today, what is the meaning of moving forward?

So, should we see it another way, when "it" refers to every shred of human knowledge and wisdom? I believe we have no choice.

We have no choice because the human journey has been defined by seeing in new ways. As suggested in these essays, little of what I believe is as it was a few years ago. Similarly, little of what we believe as a species is as it was even a few decades ago, let alone in centuries past. How arrogant to believe we have nearly exhausted the human quest for learning and wisdom! If we are nearing the end of our pursuit of wisdom, what then do we expect of the species, should we survive into the millennia ahead? Nothing new? No further insights into the meaning of existence? No new perceptions of our relationship to each other and to the biosphere? No unique, creative understanding of our lives and the life of the Universe? No new thoughts or feelings about what is beyond? If there is to be nothing new, nothing miraculous, nothing to take our collective breath away, what then for the species?

While the story of humanity has been animated by innovation and creative thought, there is a more pervasive reason why we have no choice but to see it another way. The path hewn by our current and past "wisdom" seems to have led us down a rabbit hole. Our creativity has led to unfathomable wealth (for some), unimaginable comfort (for a portion) and inconceivably complex theories about the nature of the Universe. And yet, as a global community, too many have been left far behind. We suffer from huge deficits in mental and emotional health. Millions have little edible food or potable water. We seem always to be at the brink of some new dis-ease that threatens millions or billions of humans and an uncountable number of other living organisms. We mutilate the landscape in the name of technological progress. We poison the environment and look the other way as the repercussions loom ominously.

I suggested earlier there might have been an age during which humans moved more gracefully with the rhythm of the Universe. How ironic it would be for the species to gain such deep insight into the nature of reality that we find ourselves returning to wisdom humans may have held in the millennia before we came to believe we were superior to all...masters of all we perceived.

Should we fail to see, feel and understand in profoundly new ways, I wonder if Pachamama just might choose a future without us.

Living Our Questions into the Future

"Be patient toward all that is unsolved in your heart and try to love the questions themselves, like locked rooms and

like books that are now written in a very foreign tongue. Do not now seek the answers, which cannot be given you because you would not be able to live them. And the point is, to live everything. Live the questions now. Perhaps you will then gradually, without noticing it, live along some distant day into the answer."
　　　　　　　Rainer Maria Rilke

The pages that make up this work contain more than 350 questions. Most are questions that live on in me and, I hope, within some of those to whom they were posed…and perhaps with you. I have yet to live into those answers, and suspect I never will. But, as I have tried to illustrate in this work, questions open us to new futures. When faced with a question so profound we are left in awe, we can do nothing but pause and simply be in its presence. And while it can be frightening to sit in the presence of that which is deeply unknown, when we come too quickly to an answer or conclusion because of our fear of the mysterious, we make an infinite number of futures unavailable to the generations yet unborn.

　　Is it possible the greatest wealth we can bequeath the future lies in the possibilities our fear might otherwise steal from it? I believe it is. Let us endeavor to find that path.

About the Author

Roger Breisch has lived an eclectic life.

He holds a Master of Science in Mathematics from Northern Illinois University and a Master of Science in Management from the Sloan School at MIT.

During his career he taught high school, was a manager for a Fortune 100 company, owned a management consulting company, and, most recently ran the local Chamber of Commerce.

In the midst of his professional career, Roger volunteered extensively. He chaired the local 4th of July Fireworks for 17 years, worked with teens in an anti-alcohol, anti-drug program for years, and spent more than 3000 hours (and counting) answering calls on a suicide hotline.

Roger loves challenging people to see how their thinking keeps them from finding true happiness and success, and he writes extensively. He and Judi, his wife of 35 years, have two grown children and live in Batavia, Illinois.

For more information, visit REBreisch.com or contact Roger at REBreisch@alum.mit.edu.

www.ingramcontent.com/pod-product-compliance
Lightning Source LLC
Chambersburg PA
CBHW050906160426
43194CB00011B/2306